Essential
Greek
Islands

by Mike Gerrard

Above: *Skála from Chóra on Pátmos*

PASSPORT BOOKS

NTC/Contemporary Publishing Group

Above: *Greek Orthodox priests are a familiar sight in the islands*

Front cover: *church on Thíra, man in Greek costume, Delós floor mosaic*

Back cover: *plums on Serifos*

This edition first published in 2000 by Passport Books, a division of NTC/ Contemporary Publishing Group, Inc., 4255 West Touhy Avenue, Lincolnwood (Chicago), Illinois 60712–1975 U.S.A.

The contents of this publication are believed correct at the time of printing. Nevertheless, the publishers cannot accept responsibility for errors or omissions, nor for changes in details given. We are always grateful to readers who let us know of any errors or omissions they come across, and future printings will be updated accordingly.

Published by Passport Books in conjunction with The Automobile Association of Great Britain.

Written by Mike Gerrard

Library of Congress Catalog Card Number: on file
ISBN 0-658-00632-0

Colour separation: Chroma Graphics (Overseas) Pte Ltd, Singapore

Printed and bound in Italy by Printer Trento srl

Contents

About this Book

KEY TO SYMBOLS

✚ map reference to the maps found in the What to See section

✉ address or location

☎ telephone number

🕐 opening times

🍴 restaurant or café on premises or near by

Ⓜ nearest underground train station

🚌 nearest bus/tram route

🚆 nearest overground train station

🎬 ferry crossings and boat excursions

✈ travel by air

ℹ tourist information

♿ facilities for visitors with disabilities

✋ admission charge

↔ other places of interest near by

❓ other practical information

➤ indicates the page where you will find a fuller description

---

Essential *Greek Islands* is divided into five sections to cover the most important aspects of your visit to the Greek Islands.

Viewing the Greek Islands pages 5–14
An introduction to the Greek Islands by the author.
    Features of the Greek Islands
    Essence of the Greek Islands
    The Shaping of the Greek Islands
    Peace and Quiet
    The Greek Islands' Famous

Top Ten pages 15–26
The author's choice of the Top Ten places to see in the Greek Islands, in alphabetical order, each with practical information.

What to See pages 27–90
The five main areas of the Greek Islands, each with its own brief introduction and an alphabetical listing of the main attractions.
    Practical information
    Snippets of 'Did you know…' information
    3 suggested walks
    3 suggested drives
    2 features

Where To… pages 91–116
Detailed listings of the best places to eat, stay, shop, take the children and be entertained.

Practical Matters pages 117–24
A highly visual section containing essential travel information.

Maps
All map references are to the individual maps found in the What to See section of this guide.

For example, Kefalloniá has the reference ✚ 32B2 – indicating the page on which the map is located and the grid square in which the island is to be found. A list of the maps that have been used in this travel guide can be found in the index.

Prices
Where appropriate, an indication of the cost of an establishment is given by £ signs:

£££ denotes higher prices, ££ denotes average prices, while £ denotes lower charges.

Star Ratings
Most of the places described in this book have been given a separate rating:

✪✪✪   Do not miss
✪✪   Highly recommended
✪   Worth seeing

Viewing the
Greek
Islands

Above: *spring cleaning on
Leipsoí means boats as well a
houses*
Right: *the black dress of this
woman on Lésvos indicates her
widowed status*

Mike Gerrard's Greek Islands

Filoxenía

The Greek word *filoxenía* says a lot about the Greeks. It means 'hospitality', yet it means much more than that. It is a belief in hospitality as a tradition, that a stranger is also a guest and should be treated as such. You will often hear Greeks using phrases like 'my house is your house', and they believe it. To be a guest of a Greek is to be looked after as one of the family.

Donkeys do the work in the back streets of Mandráki on Nísyros

The Greek Islands are like the Sirens of old, luring travellers to them, but never letting them go. Those making their first visit to the islands are usually in a minority, surrounded by holidaymakers who have been coming for many years. Some return to the same island year after year, while others prefer to try somewhere new, knowing that no two islands are alike and that beyond the horizon will be another gem waiting to be discovered. The islands are alike in that they all offer a glimpse of that mythical desert-island paradise, but closer to home and with most modern conveniences laid on.

My own heart is torn between returning to particular islands I have visited several times and come to know and love, such as Sými and Tílos, and uncovering new delights, of which Paxoí and Itháki are recent favourites. The answer to that dilemma, in my own case, is simply to go

as often as possible and try to do both! What is it about Greece, and in particular about the islands, that is special enough to make me return year after year? After all, you can get better food in countries such as France and Italy, and find beaches just as good all over the world. Few countries can match the historical attractions that the Greek Islands have to offer, yet that isn't the pull either. The people and their hospitality have to be high on the list of reasons for returning, and yet I have been shown many generous acts of kindness in other countries around the world. Perhaps, though, it is only in the Greek Islands where all these features combine, but that trying to define one's love for a country is as hard as analysing one's love for another person. All you know, and all that you need to know, is that it's there.

Features of the Greek Islands

Geography

There are said to be about 2,000 Greek islands, although many of these are just lumps of rock. Fewer than 200 islands are inhabited. The total area of the islands is 25,166sq km, which means that they account for about one fifth of Greece's land area. The islands range from the Ionian group off the west coast of Greece, not far from Italy, to the tiny isle of Kastellórizo, Greece's easternmost island tucked into the coast of Turkey. In the south is Crete, subject of a separate *Essential Guide*, off whose southern shore is the island of Gávdos, the most southerly point in Europe.

Climate

The main difference in climate is between the Ionian Islands in the west, and the rest of the islands, in the Aegean Sea. The Ionians are wetter, and even in summer you may not escape the odd shower, while a summer shower in the Aegean would be an extremely unusual – but possibly welcome – break from the relentless heat. Here expect summer temperatures to be in the upper 30s degrees Celsius and beyond. Winter in the islands can be bleak, not necessarily because of the cold, as many remain comparatively mild, but there will be some rain and wind, and tourist resorts may all but close down as many inhabitants prefer to live in Athens then.

Language

Greek is the official language but English is widely spoken in popular tourist areas, with Italian too, especially in the Ionian Islands. Venture off the tourist track, however, and you will need your Greek phrase book (▶ 124 for some words and phrases).

Yes and No

'No' sounds like no in many languages – *non, nein, nyet* – but in Greek *ne* means yes and no is *ohi* (pronounced *neh* and *oh-kee* or *oh-she* respectively). Further confusion can be caused by the Greek gesture for no, which can look like a nodding of the head in agreement. If someone raises their head, raises their eyebrows and sometimes adds a tutting sound, they are in fact saying no.

Even Náxos in the Aegean becomes a fertile green in spring and early summer

Essence of the Greek Islands

Above: *sweeping away the summer dust in Chómo, Kálymnos*
Below: *sun rising on the mountain village of Apéri on Kárpathos*

For some people the Greek Islands mean sunshine and beaches, but there is much more to them than a few hedonistic days in the sun. For the history-lover they are also about archaeological remains and fortresses. Those seeking solitude will discover deserted beaches on even the busiest of islands, and nature-lovers will find orchids and butterflies, birds and abundant sea life: dolphins, seals and turtles. And while Greece may not have one of the world's great cuisines, there are few finer pleasures than sitting at the waterside eating a freshly caught fish, grilled over charcoal and sprinkled with lemon juice. That taste is the essence of the Greek Islands.

THE **10** ESSENTIALS

If you only have a short time to visit the Greek Islands, or would like to get a really complete picture of them, here are the essentials:

Visit a small island, such as Psérimos (▶ 86) or Tilos (▶ 25), where tourists are fewer and the welcome is even warmer than on busier islands.

Eat at the waterside – the best of the day's catch never tastes finer than when eaten right by the sea, but be prepared to share with the neighbourhood cats!

Take a ferry ride. Some of the loveliest islands are at least one ferry ride away from the nearest airport, but even if you're not obliged to catch a ferry to get somewhere, take one anyway as an enjoyable day out. Watch the excitement that always ensues when the ferry pulls into harbour, even if it does so every day of the year.

Take a bus ride. Even the smallest islands usually have some kind of bus service, and travelling on one gives a glimpse of local life.

Drink retsina, the wine unique to Greece. Its resinous taste may not suit everyone's palate, but the inexpensive price may suit your pocket, so try it.

Learn some Greek, even if it is only the words for yes, no, please and thank you. Greeks appreciate the effort.

Understand the religion. Religious beliefs are very important to the islanders, so understand them a little more by visiting a monastery, or a church service, or by travelling at Easter.

Take a walk. It's surprising how many visitors never stray more than a few hundred metres from the nearest beach. Take a hike to the next town or village, and enjoy the scenery.

Visit a real shop – not just the souvenir shops but a genuine local shop where, floor to ceiling, the shelves are stacked with a million things.

Relax. Slow down as the Greeks do, and enjoy the passage of time and the passing show, best viewed over a cup of coffee.

Dancing is a great part of Greek life, whether informally in a taverna, or as here, at a wedding

Conversation over coffee is a daily part of Greek life, as here in Skyros Town

9

The Shaping of the Greek Islands

3000 BC
The first signs of culture emerge in the Cyclades, where Bronze Age sea traders settle.

2200–1700
The Minoan civilisation on Crete develops.

1700–1600
The Mycenean civilisation develops on the mainland and then spreads to the Greek Islands.

c1470
Volcanic explosion on Thíra wipes out Minoan civilisation.

800–600
The first city states emerge, including Athens.

478
Domination of the Islands

The lions at Delos are a reminder of the wealth of ancient Greece

by Athens, as leader of the Delian League, begins.

200 BC–AD 300
The Romans conquer and rule Greece.

AD 324
Emperor Constantine establishes Constantinople (formerly Byzantium) as the capital of the eastern part of the Roman Empire.

1204
The Venetians and Franks take Constantinople and divide Greece between them, including Crete, the Ionian Islands and the Dodecanese.

1261–2
The Byzantine Empire retakes Constantinople and much of mainland Greece.

1453
The fall of Constantinople (Istanbul) and the end of the Byzantine Empire.

1453–1821
Greece is under Turkish rule.

1522
The Turks capture Rhodes.

1566
The Turks take Chíos and Náxos.

1571
The Turks capture Sámos.

1797
France captures the Ionian Islands from the Venetians.

1814–64
Britain captures and rules the Ionian Islands.

1821–9
The Greek War of Independence.

1832
Prince Otto of Bavaria elected the first king of the modern Greek state.

1864
The Ionian Islands are returned to Greece.

1912
The First Balkan War: Greece recaptures Chíos from the Ottoman Empire, but Italy takes the Dodecanese.

1913
The Second Balkan War: Greece takes Lésvos, Sámos and Ikaría.

1917
Greece enters World War I on the side of the Allies.

1920–3
Greece wages an ill-judged war against Turkey, ending in humiliating defeat.

1923
The exchange of populations, when one million Greeks in Turkey are forced back to their homeland, while 400,000 Muslims have to leave Greece for Turkey.

1940
In World War II Mussolini demands access to Greek ports, which the Greek general Metaxas refuses in a word: 'No'.

1944
The Allies liberate Greece.

1944–9
A civil war rages between communist and right-wing Government forces.

1947
The Dodecanese are handed back to Greece.

1951
Greece joins NATO.

1952
Greek women receive the vote.

1953
A major earthquake devastates the Ionian Islands.

An engraving from 1480 shows the invading Turks' Siege of Rhodes

1967
A military junta seizes power and King Constantine flees into exile. Rule of the Colonels starts, under Colonel Papadopoulos.

1974
The junta is overthrown and democracy returns.

1975
A new republican constitution means the end of the monarchy.

1981
Greece joins the EC.

1988
Terrorists attack *City of Poros* excursion boat.

1996
PASOK leader Andréas Papandréou dies.

11

Peace & Quiet

Loggerhead turtles nest on some of the Islands' finest beaches

Red Blobs
Greece does not have a large network of well waymarked footpaths, as many countries do. It does have the paths, but in areas where they are difficult to follow you are likely to find no more than a series of blobs of red paint on rocks and walls, to indicate which way you should go.

Stripping Off
If you find a peaceful and remote beach, you may well want to strip off and sunbathe in the nude. There are a few official nudist beaches in the islands, but elsewhere it is illegal to undress completely. However, if you are in a remote place and in no danger of offending anyone, it is unlikely you will face problems – well, problems other than sunburn, that is.

Where to Go

Busy islands such as Corfu (➤ 34), Kós (➤ 82) and Rhodes (➤ 88) are still big enough to have many quiet resorts and deserted beaches. If you want guaranteed peace and quiet, though, you must choose your base carefully. The southern tip of Corfu might look remote, with few villages, but one of its resorts, Kávos, is renowned for its noisy nightlife. On the other hand, the southern tip of Rhodes is scarcely developed yet for tourism, in complete contrast to the northern tip which has become one huge beach resort.

To be sure of a peaceful time, choose one of the smaller islands. These days, it is not only the islands with airports that are busy, but also the islands around them which are just a short ferry ride away. Most package holidaymakers want to leave home and arrive in their resort on the same day, so there is a limit to how far they will travel. Choose an island that requires two ferry trips to get to it, or a ferry ride of at least four hours, and you will probably see few other tourists.

When to Go

The Greek Islands are really only very busy in the peak season from late June into early September. Outside those times the pressure is off, and if you travel in spring or autumn you will probably have fine weather, and a feeling of freedom. The Ionian Islands tend to be wetter, so if it's sunny weather you seek then consider the Cyclades or Dodecanese for out-of-season travelling. In April and May you will see the spring flowers and migrating birds, and in October you will see peace return to the islands as the migrating summer visitors, known as tourists, have mostly gone home.

Wildlife Havens

Although many visitors head for the Greek Islands for the nightlife, places such as Corfu, Kós and Rhodes are still home to plenty of wildlife, proof that peace and quiet can also be found there. Only occasionally do the needs of visitors and of nature conflict, causing problems such as have occurred on the beach at Laganás on Zákynthos (➤ 41), where sunbathers and loggerhead turtles find the same long stretch of sand equally attractive. Elsewhere,

man and nature usually manage to live in harmony, and there is no Greek island where some peace and quiet cannot be found.

Even what was once regarded as the most developed island of them all, Corfu, has unspoilt areas that other Mediterranean places can only dream about. Here you will still find – if you are lucky enough to see one – some of the last few hundred Mediterranean monk seals in existence. On the north of the island, by the Andinioti Lagoon, you will find several species of heron, marsh harriers and nightingales.

Olive groves provide welcome shade when exploring away from the tourist areas

Marsh harriers are often seen above the Andinioti Lagoon on Corfu

Lésvos

As the third largest Greek island, Lésvos (► 18) has plenty of room for peaceful escape. The coastal resort of Skála Kallonís manages to combine package holidays with birdwatching, as ornithologists gather here to enjoy the neighbouring salt marshes, especially in April and May. Further west, resorts are fewer and escape from the crowds easier. A rare species that may be seen on Lésvos and down the eastern side of the Aegean Sea is Eleonora's falcon, one of the rarest birds of prey in the world and the only one which lives communally. If you see flocks of what appear to be large swallows hunting insects in the sky at dusk, you may well be seeing not swallows but falcons.

The Greek Islands' Famous

Greek Poetic Tradition
For such a small country Greece has a long and distinguished tradition of great poetry, which continues today. Odysseus Elytis (born on Lésvos) won the Nobel Prize for Literature in 1979, following on from George Seferis, who won the same prize in 1963.

Pythagoras

Pythagoras was born on the island of Sámos in about 580 BC. Nowadays he is perhaps best known as a mathematician, and in particular for his theorem, which states that in a right-angled triangle the square of the longest side is equal to the sum of the squares of the other two sides. His knowledge of mathematics led him to believe that numbers were the key to the understanding of the whole of the natural world and he was also famous as a philosopher, as the discoverer of the mathematical basis of musical harmony, and as an astronomer. He held that the earth and the universe were spherical, and that the sun, the moon, and the planets had a rotation of their own. His followers, the Pythagoreans, went on to develop the system that the earth was not the centre of the universe but merely one of the planets that revolved around the sun. He left Sámos in about 530 BC to escape the tyrannical rule of Polycrates, and settled with his followers in the Greek colony of Crotona in southern Italy. He died in about 500 BC.

Sappho is one in a long line of Greek poets which extends to the present day

Sappho

The Greek poet Sappho was born on the island of Lésvos in about 650 BC, probably in the main town of Mytilíni, although the village of Eresós also claims to be her birthplace. Although she gave her name to the notion of 'Sapphic Love', and her native island provided the word 'lesbian', there is no certain evidence that Sappho was lesbian herself. She appears to have come from a noble family, to have had several lovers including the equally renowned male poet Alcaeus, and then to have married and had a daughter named Cleïs. The lesbian assertions were made by a later poet, Anacreon, who claimed that Sappho felt a sexual love for the women students that she taught. Only fragments of her poetry remain, but we know that she was held in such high esteem that the philosopher Plato described her as the Tenth Muse. She died in about 590 BC.

Top Ten

Above: *restored houses in Oia on picturesque Thíra*
Right: *religious heritage displayed in a golden mosaic from Pátmos*

15

1
Kárpathos

🕂 74C1

☎ Tourist Police (Pigádia):
0245 22222; Airport
Information: 0245
22058

Twice weekly to
Rhodes Town, weekly
to Athens, Crete, and
some Dodecanesian
and Cycladic islands

❓ Daily trips in season
from Pigádia to
Ólympos, by bus or
boat

*Windmills, like this one
at Ólympos, are a
common sight*

*Kárpathos is one of the most traditional Greek
Islands, rugged and mountainous, where tourism
has only recently started to make inroads.*

The third largest island in the Dodecanese group,
Kárpathos is a long, thin strip of mountainous land whose
peaks reach a height of over 1,200m. This rough, hilly
spine makes for quite a distinction between the more
mountainous north of the island and the lower-lying south.
It is in the south where most of the population lives, and
where tourist development has started to make an impact
over the last few years. Even so, it is far less affected by
tourism than other islands of comparable size, and visitors
will appreciate the more traditional way of life.

The island now has an airport but only for domestic
flights, with several connections per week to Athens and
Rhodes. Not far from the airport is the capital, Pigádia, also
known as Kárpathos Town. It is a typical modern Greek
port in a beautiful setting on Vróndi Bay, where a sweep of
sand runs for 3km to the north of the town. Pigádia's old
fishing harbour is also a picturesque spot to while away
some time over a coffee or a meal at one of the waterside
tavernas.

Visitors must go and see some of the lovely mountain
villages, such as Apéri and Óthos, both easily reached
from the capital, although the big draw is the traditional
village of Ólympos, in the north of the island. This is harder
to reach but day trips can be arranged from the capital or
the handful of beach resorts that now exist. Many of the
women in Ólympos still wear colourful traditional
costumes, and the village's whitewashed houses cling to
the steep slopes of the surrounding mountains, where
ruined windmills add to the picturesque scene.

2
Kefalloniá

Kefalloniá is the largest of the seven Ionian Islands. It has long been a popular tourist destination, but its size ensures that there is still plenty of room.

Greeks as well as foreigners come to holiday on Kefalloniá, taking advantage of its impressive beaches, pine-clad hills and its mix of busy resorts with quieter places. Numbers have increased recently since the success of Louis de Bernière's novel, *Captain Corelli's Mandolin*, which is set on the island during the Italian wartime occupation. Not long after this period, a terrible earthquake in 1953 wiped out many of its towns and villages, and the scale of the disaster can be appreciated by visiting the **Historical and Cultural Museum** in the capital town, Argostóli. Amongst many interesting displays of costumes, jewellery and other island artifacts are photographs taken before and immediately after the quake, showing the utter devastation it brought. Argostóli was rebuilt, and despite its modernity is an attractive town on a bay, with some waterfront tavernas where you can enjoy the best of the day's catch, bought from the fishermen along the harbour.

One town that escaped the quake's damage is Fiskárdo, on the northern tip of the island. It still has its colourful 18th-century mansions overlooking a pretty little harbour, and is usually crowded with visitors in high season – but who can blame them? Half-way along the western side of the island is Mírtos Beach, a stunning curve of white-pebbled beach around a bay whose waters are frequently a deep turquoise colour. It is such an impressive sight that it is used again and again on advertising posters for the Greek Islands. Kefalloniá's other natural attractions include the 30,000-year-old Melissáni Cave, the nearby Drogaráti Cave and the National Park around Mount Énos (1,628m).

✚ 32B2

ℹ Tourist Office:
B Customs Pier,
Argostóli ☎ 0671 22248

⛴ Daily ferries to Pátra on mainland, and to other Ionian islands, from Sámi, Póros, Fiskárdo or Pessáda

Historical and Cultural Museum

✉ Ilía Zervoú, Argostóli

🕐 Tue–Sun 8:30–3:30

Kefalloniá's deep blue coastal waters

3
Lésvos

 47C3

Aristárkhou 6, Mytilíni
☎ 1251 42511; Tourist
Police ☎ 0251 2277

Several per week from
Mytilíni to Athens,
Chíos, Límnos, less
frequently to
Thessaloníki, Kavála,
Rafína, Vólos and some
islands

Theophilos Museum

 Odós Mikras Asias,
Variá

☎ 0251 41644

🕐 Tue–Sun 9–1, 4:30–10

Archaeological Museum

✉ Odós Argíri Eftalídi 7,
Mytilíni

☎ 0251 28032

🕐 Tue–Sun 8:30–3

*Houses in Mólyvos
cluster beneath the
imposing Genoese castle*

*The third largest Greek island , Lésvos has always
been a popular holiday spot for Greeks, and now
many foreign visitors also enjoy its attractions.*

Lésvos was always a prosperous island long before
tourism came on the scene. It was a centre for ship-
building, and is said to produce some of the best ouzo in
Greece. Its fertile interior – hilly rather than mountainous –
is especially good for olive-growing, and there is a great
deal of grain production and fishing too. It has also
produced a good crop of artists over the years, from
Sappho (▶14) and Aesop through to the modern Nobel
laureate, Odysseus Elýtis. Other artistic islanders include
the modern Greek novelist, Stratis Myrivilis, whose books
can be found everywhere, and the primitive artist,
Theophilos. There is a **Theophilos Museum** in Variá, not
far from the busy capital, the port of Mytilíni. While this
has a good **Archaeological Museum**, conveniently close
to the ferries if you have time to spare, Mytilíni is mainly a
gateway to the many other more attractive places on
Lésvos.

Mólyvos is the main tourist centre in the north of the
island, and despite its popularity it has managed to retain
its charm. It is built around a Genoese castle, and many of
its cobbled streets are shaded by vines, and below the
castle is a lovely little fishing harbour. Beach fanatics may
prefer the growing resort of Pétra, just south of Mólyvos.

In western Lésvos are two other popular and attractive

destinations. The village of
Eresós is where the poet
Sappho is believed to have
been born (▶14). The
connection makes it very
popular with lesbian visitors
who combine homage with
hedonism on its beautiful
long beach. Further west still
is Sígri, with another
appealing beach and a
handful of hotels and
tavernas. Sígri retains the feel
of a village community, rather
than somewhere that has
turned into a beach resort,
just as Lésvos manages to
retain its Greekness, despite
the onslaught of mass
tourism.

4
Mýkonos

The windmills and white houses of Mýkonos have featured on many postcards, and it is now one of the most cosmopolitan of all the Aegean islands.

Travellers have come to Mýkonos for thousands of years, as it was the gateway to the sacred island of Dílos (▶ 62), and this remains the case today as no one is allowed to stay on Dílos. However, nowadays visitors come to Mýkonos for a great number of other reasons, as evidenced by the fact that it is one of the most visited of all the Greek islands, with about 800,000 tourists a year. Most visitors come for the beaches and the summer nightlife, which is as loud and as rowdy as anywhere in the Mediterranean, with a particular appeal to gay travellers. This has lessened in recent years, but is still very much in evidence. Other visitors come because it is one of the few places in Greece where scuba diving is permitted, and many of the beaches have diving centres.

If you don't like your islands too crowded, Mýkonos is best enjoyed slightly out of season, when the sun still shines but the beaches are less busy. The popularity of the island does mean that it has a more prosperous air, and that tourist facilities are generally good, with eating places to match, though prices can be somewhat higher. Mýkonos Town has a busy port area but a quieter harbour and several museums worth visiting: **Archaeological**, **Marine** and **Folklore**. Its familiar windmills can be found on the hillside in the area known as Little Venice, after the elegant Venetian-style houses. The main town tends to dominate Mýkonos, as the island's villages are all quite small, but Agía Ánna is a popular spot to visit, as this was the setting for the film *Shirley Valentine*.

✝ 59D4

ℹ Tourist Police ☎ 0289 22482; Post Office ☎ 0289 22238

⛴ At least two per day to Athens, Tínos, Ándros and Sýros, less frequently to most Cycladic and Dodecanesian islands, and beyond

? Day trips to Dílos (▶ 62) leave from the harbour at Mýkonos Town, several per day

Archaeological Museum

✉ Quayside, Mýkonos Town

☎ 0289 22325

🕐 Tue–Sat 9:30–3, Sun 9:30–2:30

Marine Museum

✉ Enopíon, Dynámeon, Mýkonos Town

☎ 0289 22700

🕐 Tue–Sun 8:30–3

Folklore Museum

✉ Quayside, Mýkonos Town

☎ 0289 22591

🕐 Mon–Sat 5:30–8:30, Sun 6:30–8:30

The picturesque, narrow streets of Mýkonos also keep out the worst of the fierce sun

19

5
Pátmos

 74A6

 Tourist Office ☎ 0247 31666/31158

Daily to Athens, Kálymnos, Kós, Léros and Rhodes, 2–3 per week to other islands

Monastery of St John

✉ Chóra

☎ 0247 31398

🕐 Daily 8–2 and also 4–6 Sun, Tue, Thu

Monastery of the Apocalypse

✉ Between Chóra and Skála

☎ 0247 31234

🕐 Daily 8–2 and also 4–6 Mon, Wed, Fri

Monks at work in the Treasury of the Monastery of St John, Pátmos

Pátmos is where St John the Divine is said to have received his 'Revelation'. Today visitors come both on pilgrimage and to enjoy its excellent beaches.

In 1088 the **Monastery of St John** was founded to commemorate the holy visions of the saint, just one of over forty churches and monasteries in Pátmos Town alone. It was built as a fortress to protect it from pirates, and although not all of it is open to visitors, it is an essential visit, particularly for the sumptuous displays of religious items housed in its Treasury. The old town, also known as Chóra, stands on and around a clifftop looking down on the port, also known as Skála. Midway between these two centres is the **Monastery of the Apocalypse**, which was built around the cave where St John the Divine is said to have heard the voice of God from a split in the rock. In summer coaches take day-trippers from Skála up to Chóra and back, and Pátmos may not then seem like the holiest of places, but once the visitors have left, and out of season, the island's essential Greekness returns.

The village of Grígos is the main tourist development, though by far the best beach is at Psilí Ámmos, a beautiful strip of shaded sand which can be reached by boat from Skála. Also popular for its rainbow array of coloured pebbles is Lámpi, but there are any number of other quiet beaches, where the visitors thronging to the two main monasteries never venture.

6
Paxoí

Although only a short ferry ride from the busy island of Corfu, Paxoí, with its handful of villages, has retained its charm and character.

The pretty and peaceful harbour in the village of Lákka on Paxoí

Part of Paxoí's appeal is that it is so small – you could walk from end to end in an afternoon – that visitors quickly feel that they get to know the place. No matter which of the three main tourist centres you stay in, your face will soon become familiar to the locals, who are friendlier than on many islands as they have not yet been swamped with tourists. That is not to say that it is totally quiet, as the three villages have their regular devotees, and Greek voices are certainly outnumbered by other European accents in high season. The capital, Gáïos, clusters round a crescent-shaped harbour and is the main point of arrival. Two tiny islands stand in its bay, on one of which are the remains of a 15th-century Venetian fortress, though Gáïos doesn't give the impression of having been much affected by any major events in history.

Most visitors stay in one or other of the two remaining villages. Longós (pronounced Loggos) hardly merits a mention in many guidebooks and its regular devotees will be quite happy with that, content to keep its charms to themselves. Life goes on around a busy little harbour, where waterfront tavernas dish up some of the best food in the Ionian islands, a testimony to Paxoí's fertility – it is said to produce some of the best olive oil in Greece.

Finally, at the northern tip of the island is Lákka, set around another idyllic bay with beaches nearby but with nothing as modern as a bank or a post office. And that, of course, is all part of the charm of Paxoí.

Off Paxoí is the even smaller island of Antipaxoí, which you can visit on a day trip from the harbour at Gáïos. With only two summer tavernas and no shops, you would need to be well-provisioned to stay there, although there are a few villas to rent if you ask in the travel agencies in Gáïos.

✚ 32B4

ℹ Port Authority ☎ 0662 31259; Police ☎ 0662 31222

🚢 Daily connections with Corfu in season, weekly out of season

❓ Day trips from Gáïos to Antipaxoí in season

21

7
Sými

75D4

Police ☎ 0241 71111;
Post Office ☎ 0241
71315 (both in same
building next to clock
tower on waterfront)

Excursion boats daily
from Rhodes,
passenger ferry weekly
to Rhodes, Athens and
other Dodecanesian and
Cycladic islands

*Sými is a true jewel of the Aegean, a miniature
beauty of an island which seems to work its magic
spell on everyone who visits it.*

Most visitors reach Sými on the two-hour ferry trip from
Rhodes – either to stay or on a day trip – but it is increasingly popular with the sailing fraternity, as its busy little
harbour demonstrates. Those lucky enough to travel on
the evening ferry, who arrive at Sými's harbour at dusk or
after nightfall, will have an experience they will never
forget. As the boat rounds the headland into the
horseshoe-shaped harbour, you are greeted by the lights
of the houses on the hillsides that slope steeply down to
the waterfront, as if sailing into a fairy grotto. Not many
years ago this was a sight only seen by the few devotees
who had discovered Sými's delights, for even though it is
so close to the busy island of Rhodes, Sými itself
remained relatively undeveloped. It would spring to life at
mid-morning when the ferries brought over the first day-
trippers, selling them souvenirs and serving them meals in
the tavernas that line the waterfront, and then return to its
own sleepy ways by late afternoon.

*A visit to the monastery
at Panormítis is a popular
day trip from Sými Town*

Today it attracts holidaymakers in
its own right, as well as having an
increased population as more of its
ruined mansions are restored. Small
yachts and big boats are also using
its harbour in growing numbers, and
as a result sleepy Sými has become
fairly chic Sými, with fashionable
bars and shops opening their doors.
If you are there during midsummer
at mid-morning, when the ferries
from Rhodes honk their way into the
harbour and disgorge several
hundred visitors, the old Sými can
seem a very long way away. The
island deserves its modern
prosperity though, as at one time it
was very wealthy indeed, thanks to
two main industries: sponge-fishing
and boat-building. Remnants of both
can still be seen, in the shops selling
sponges along the harbour, and in
the handful of remaining boat-
builders between the harbour and
the small town beach, but it is hard
to imagine that it once had a

population of some 30,000, even more than its big neighbour, Rhodes.

Some of the mansions that housed these people can be seen as you climb the steep streets between the harbour, Yialós, and the upper old town, Chorió. Many have been splendidly restored and must make wonderful homes with their views over the harbour, while others are still in a state of magnificent crumbling decay. Sými's small but enjoyable local **museum** is also in Chorió, which is much quieter than the harbour area, and it's possible to become pleasurably lost as you wander round the maze of streets.

If you do make your way through to the other side, a road leads down to the popular beach at Pédi, while walking along the coast from Yialós in the opposite direction takes you to Emporeió. Here there is another small beach and a good taverna, though there are other small coves that can be reached by climbing down from the coastal road.

At the southern end of the island, and a popular day trip, is the **Monastery of Panormítis**, with a lovely courtyard, idiosyncratic museum, and a real feeling of peace – if you don't coincide with one of the ferry trips from Rhodes.

Sými Museum

 Chorió, Sými Town

☎ 0241 71114

🕐 Tue–Sun 10–2

Panormítis Monastery

✉ Panormítis Bay

🕐 Daily 11–12, 2:30–4

The harbour at Sými is one of the most beautiful in the Aegean

8
Thíra (Santoríni)

Oía on Thíra is perched dramatically on the rim of the crater

No island is quite like Thíra, with its dazzling white houses perched dramatically on the cliffs around a flooded volcanic crater.

In about 1450 BC the volcanic island of Thíra erupted in spectacular fashion, resulting in half the island sinking beneath the waves. It is thought that a sequence of tremors and tidal waves then spread as far as Crete, destroying the Minoan civilisation there. Thíra itself had been conquered by the Minoans in 3000 BC, and its destruction ensured that it was one candidate for the fabled lost city of Atlantis. One result of the volcanic past is that Thíra's beaches are today composed of ash-black sand or pebbles, striking to look at but also incredibly hot in summer. The island is also extremely busy then, and the charms of its main town, also known as Thíra (sometimes Fíra or Chóra) are best appreciated slightly out of season. It is a cosmopolitan and quite expensive place by Greek standards, but an essential visit for its unique clifftop location. It must be one of the most stunning settings in the world in which to enjoy a drink at sunset.

Thíra's other major attractions without which no visit is complete include the ruined Minoan city of **Akrotíri**, the island's ancient capital of **Archaía Thíra** (Ancient Thíra), the village of Oía, which has the loveliest setting on the island, and the **Archaeological Museum** in Thíra Town. The best frescoes discovered in excavating the sites on Thíra have been put on display in the National Archaeological Museum in Athens, but this museum on the island itself still gives a good background to the turbulent history of this unique place.

 59D1

 Tourist Police ☎ 0286 22649

Daily to Athens, Crete, Páros, Íos, Náxos, several per week to other islands

Akrotíri
🕐 Tue–Sat 8:30–3

Archaía Thíra
🕐 Tue–Sun 9–3

Archaeological Museum
✉ Opposite the cable-car station, Thíra Town
🕐 Tue–Sun 8:30–3

9
Tílos

Tiny Tílos is the kind of island you thought didn't exist – relatively undiscovered, with good places to eat, a wonderful little hotel, yet unspoilt.

The island bus awaits the ferry arrival – a big event on quiet Tílos

One thing that has kept Tílos from being too overrun by visitors (and even in midsummer the numbers are comparatively small) is its relative inaccessibility. There are ferries once or twice a week linking it with Athens and Rhodes, but many package tourists are discouraged by the lengthy transfer of four hours by ferry or two hours by hydrofoil from the nearest airport at Rhodes. This works to the advantage of those who like their Greek islands peaceful.

Tílos has no major tourist attractions, and while its hilly landscape is pleasant enough, it is not spectacular. However, its people are wonderfully welcoming, and extremely hospitable to those who choose to stay on their island. The port and main village of Livádia is the kind of place, all too rare these days, where you can sit in the village square in the evening alongside the locals, watching the children playing around the fountain, and sipping a coffee or an ouzo as the sun goes down. Livádia has a handful of good tavernas, a few hotels and rooms to rent, a beach close to the town and other beaches a short walk away along the coastal paths. A bus makes irregular journeys to the island's second village, Megálo Chorió, set below the ruins of one of several Venetian castles that somehow manage to fit onto this little island. Tílos's third village, Mikró Chorió, is now deserted except on some summer evenings when locals and tourists drive to the recently renovated disco-pub. This relaxing mix of local life and tourism is what gives Tílos its lovely lazy charm.

🕂 74C4

ℹ Port Authority ☎ 0241 44350

Weekly to Athens, Rhodes and other Dodecanesian and some Cycladic islands

25

10
Ýdra

28C2

Port Authority ☎ 0298
52279; Tourist Police
☎ 0298 52205

Many daily ferries/
hydrofoils from Athens
and the other Argo-
Saronic islands, with
regular connections to
the Greek mainland

*Ýdra was one of the first islands to be discovered by
visitors in any numbers. It is now one of the most
sophisticated of island destinations.*

Ýdra has always been a prosperous island, as its many fine
houses testify. These tall stone mansions were mostly
built in the 19th century by ship-builders, merchants and
sea captains, at a time when Ýdra boasted one of the
biggest fleets of sailing ships in the whole of Greece. It is
hard to believe when you look at this fairly small island, but
it once housed a population of some 25,000 people. When
the shipping industry died out in the 1950s and 1960s the
island was discovered anew by artists and writers, some
of whom renovated the mansions, opened galleries or
simply hung out and relaxed. They created a Bohemian
atmosphere in a kind of Greek version of St Tropez, with
boutiques, cafés, galleries and restaurants attracting
visitors from Athens, day-trippers from other islands and
flotillas of yachts. There seems to be no let-up in Ýdra's
appeal, as more recently bars, *ouzéris* and nightclubs have
added to the international atmosphere.

This is not, of course, to everyone's taste, but if you like
your Greek islands with a bit of life to them, Ýdra is
definitely one of the main options. However, the ban on
traffic definitely adds to its appeal. It is also relatively easy
to escape from the crowds by wandering along the coastal
tracks to quiet, unspoilt beaches, or inland to see the
Monastery of Profítis Ilías and the Convent of Agía
Efpraxía. Further on is the Monastery of Agía Triáda,
where only men may visit.

*This smart boutique is
typical of the shops
around Ýdra*

What to See

Above: *a donkey grazes outside Chóra on Pátmos*
Right: *a kindly priest from the island of Rhodes*

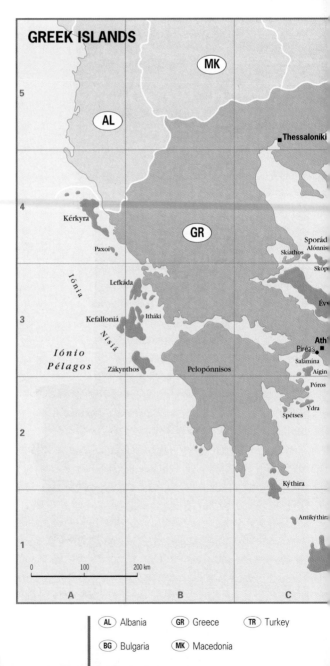

BG

Thásos

Samothráki

Límnos

Ágios
Efstrátios

oúra

Aigaio

Pélagos

Skýros

Lésvos

Chíos

TR

Psará

Ándros

Sámos

Kéa

Tínos

Ikaría

Foúrnoi

Sýros

Mýkonos

Arkoí

Agathónisi

hnos

Kykládes

Dílos

Pátmos

Leipsoí

fos

Páros

Donoússa

Léros

Sífnos

Náxos

Kálymnos

Dodekánisos

Antíparos

Kós

Síkinos

Íos

Amorgós

ilos

Folégandros

Astypálaia

Nísyros

Tílos

Sými

Thíra
(Santoríni)

Anáfi

Chálki

Ródos

Kritikó Pélagos

Kárpathos

Kásos

Kríti

ydos

D

E

F

Ionian Islands

For any traveller whose impression of the Greek Islands has been gained from the Aegean, the first sight of the much lusher Ionian Islands can be quite a surprise. This group of seven islands which stretches down the west coast of Greece from Kérkyra (better known as Corfu) to Kýthira (hardly known at all) experiences heavier rainfall, to the benefit of the olive groves, vineyards and orchards – and the golf course on Corfu.

Corfu gained a reputation as an island ruined by tourism, descended on annually by European youth out for a good time. While the island still attracts some such visitors, it is also a place where you can find traditional Greek hospitality, quiet villages and beautiful beaches. Paxoí to the south is a tiny olive-filled island of just three main villages. The southernmost island of Kýthira is actually closer to Crete than to its Ionian neighbours, and perhaps also closer to the true Greek spirit.

> *' From the steep prow I marked
> with quickening eye
> Zákynthos, every olive grove
> and creek,
> Ithaca's cliff, Lycaon's snowy
> peak… '*

OSCAR WILDE (1854–1900),
Impression du Voyage

———————●———————

The 16th-century Cathedral of the Panagía Spiliotissa, Corfu Town

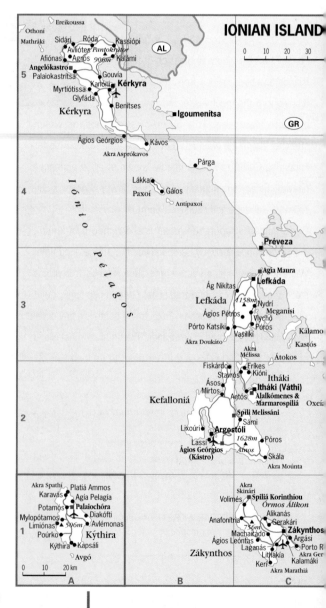

IONIAN ISLAND

0   10   20   30

What to See in the Ionian Islands

ITHÁKI ✪✪✪

Ith's is astonishingly unspoilt, given that it is tucked up close against its busy big neighbour, Kefalloniá, and is only a short ferry ride from Lefkáda which connects with the mainland. Its main claim to fame has always been its status as the legendary home of Odysseus, the place to which the hero spent many long years trying to return, as described in Homer's *The Odyssey*. There is no hard evidence for this, but there is plenty of fun to be had in trying to match locations described in the book with the real world of Ith's. A map available on the island will point you in the right direction for such alleged sites as the Castle of Odysseus, the Cave of the Nymphs and the Arethoúsa Spring.

As for real locations, the island's capital is Váthi, marvellously located at the end of a long bay, which is itself off a larger bay, the Molos Gulf. It is a pleasantly relaxed place, not at all like the bustling ports of larger Greek islands. A few of its fine mansions survived the earthquake which devastated much of the Ionian islands in 1953, and there is a cathedral, a small **Archaeological Museum**, a church which contains an icon attributed to El Greco, and some good beaches on the edge of the town.

The rest of the island is made up of a scattering of villages, with a small tourist development at Fríkes in the north of Ithás, where ferries from Lefkáda and Kefalloniá call in. Along the coast is Kióni, another small beach resort with rooms to rent and places to eat, but as low key as the rest of Ithás.

KEFALLONIÁ (➤ 17, TOP TEN)

➕ 32C2

Daily to Kefalloniá and Lefkáda, and to Astakós and Pátra on the mainland

Archaeological Museum

✉ Kallinískou, Váthi

☎ 0674 32200

🕐 Tue–Sun, 8:30–2

♿ Good

🎫 Free

Boats in the harbour at Fríkes, on Ithás

+ 32A5

ℹ️ Vouléfton, Corfu Town
☎ 0661 37520/37638
🕐 Mon–Fri 8–2; Tourist
Police ✉ Arseníou 31,
Corfu Town ☎ 0661
30265

🚢 Daily to Igoumenítsa and
Pátra (mainland) and to
Paxoí (in season), less
frequent to Kefalloniá

Archaeological Museum
✉ Vráilal, Corfu Town
☎ 0661 30680
🕐 Tue–Sun 8:30–3

Achilleion Palace
✉ 19km southwest of Corfu
Town
☎ 0661 56210
🕐 Daily 9–3

Above: *The resort of
Palaiokastrítsa is one of
the prettiest on Corfu*

KÉRKYRA (CORFU)   ✪✪✪

Corfu is the best known of the Ionian islands, although not always for the right reasons. It was the first to cater for mass-market tourism, as a result of which several resorts were quickly built and became the ugly face of holiday development. It was also known as the place where rowdy youngsters went in search of a good time, with little regard for their hosts or their fellow tourists. A lot of that has now changed, however, and like many other Mediterranean destinations Corfu realised the long-term benefits of appealing to more discerning travellers, as well as to the family holiday market. There are still busy and brash resorts, such as Kávos and the long-time favourite Benítses, but the island is big enough to accommodate much else besides.

Corfu Town, for instance, has some magnificent buildings as a result of its mixed past, particularly influenced by the Venetians, the French and the British. Its Old Town is a wonderful place to wander around, with traffic-free narrow back streets and some very up-market shopping reflecting the prosperity that tourism has brought to the island.

Elsewhere on the island there is some breathtaking scenery, such as the 906m high peak of Mount Pantokrátor and the popular resort of Palaiokastrítsa, which clusters round a wooded headland and is one of the loveliest places on the whole island. Further down the west coast is the beach of Myrtiótissa, which was described by writer Lawrence Durrell as 'perhaps the loveliest beach in the world'.

DID YOU KNOW?

There are between 3 and 4 million olive trees on Corfu. Corfiots have been cultivating the olive for 5,000 years, but they do so in an unusual manner. They do not pick the fruit or beat the branches with sticks, but let the olives fall to the ground naturally. Nor do they prune their trees. The result is that they have some of the largest trees in Greece. An unusual feature of the olive tree in Greece is that it may be owned by someone other than the owner of the land it stands on, although the landowner must allow access.

Exploring Northern Corfu

This day-long drive explores the mountain villages of northern Corfu, without neglecting its beaches.

Leave Corfu Town on the northern coast road, passing the resorts of Kondókali and Gouvía. Beyond Gouvía turn left for Palaiokastrítsa.

The road goes through a wooded valley, with the bulk of Mount Pantokrátor (906m) away to the right.

About 2km beyond Sgombou take the right turn marked Sidári. Follow this road to the Troumpéta Pass with wonderful views to the left of the Rópa Plain of central Corfu. At Troumpéta take the right turn towards Róda, passing through the villages of Khorepískopi, Valanió, Kiprianádes, Xanthátai, Plátonas and Sfakerá. Beyond this last village you reach the main road, where you turn left towards Karousádes and Sidári.

Sidári is a lively beach resort, well worth a break to stretch the legs, have lunch and see its unusual rock formations, especially the Canal d'Amour.

Continue on the coastal road, past a viewpoint at Avlióles, through Aríllas, and about 2km beyond here turn left on the Sidári road.

At Kavadádes you might want to break the journey to walk up to another fine viewpoint, showing the very best of this northwestern hill scenery.

At Kavadádes turn right to Armenádes, where you turn right again through Dafní (where there is a petrol station) and on through Agrós and back to the Troumpéta Pass, where you pick up the road you drove up on, this time heading back down towards Corfu Town.

Distance
100km

Time
6–7 hours

Start/end point
Corfu Town

Lunch
Nicholas (££)
✉ Canal d'Amour, Perouládes, Sidári
☎ 0663 95213

A winding road leads to Corfu's highest point, Mount Pantokrátor

Food & Drink

One thing visitors to the Greek islands are guaranteed is a splendid setting in which to enjoy Greek food, with waterfront tavernas in abundance. While Greek menus may not be as varied or sophisticated as those in some other Mediterranean countries, they still offer some of the best-value food, and some of the freshest fish, you can buy anywhere.

Kumquat
If you see a tree on Corfu which appears to be growing lemon-shaped oranges, it is probably a kumquat. Originating in Asia, this tree was introduced to Corfu and to Sicily, the only two places in the Mediterranean where it flourishes. The fruit is turned into a jam as well as being made into a sweet-tasting liqueur, both of which make good souvenirs.

Tomatoes hung up to dry in the sun

When to Eat
One thing the Greeks do have in common with other Mediterranean countries is a tendency to eat late. Lunch seldom starts before about 2PM and will spread into the afternoon, although tavernas in tourist areas will be open much earlier and be ready for the earlier dining habits of visitors. In the evening, places will usually be open from about 7PM onwards, but it will be at least another hour or two before the Greeks start to think about eating.

Starters
Greek meals often start with a dip, or several dips, such as *taramasalata* (fish roe), *tsatsiki* (yoghourt, garlic and cucumber) or *melitzanasalata* (aubergine dip). Other favourites include *dolmades* (stuffed vine leaves) and deep-fried vegetables such as courgettes or aubergines. If you have a hearty appetite or are dining in a group, you might want to order a *meze*, which is a mixed selection of starters.

Fish
Fresh fish is one of the treats of the Greek islands, and the usual cooking method is simply to grill it over charcoal and serve it with a slice of lemon. In most tavernas you are very welcome – in fact expected – to go into the kitchen and choose your fish. Be aware that the price on the menu is usually per kilo, not per fish, so don't be afraid to ask for the fish to be weighed and priced before you choose.

Hot Dishes
With such a hot climate to cope with in summer, the Greeks are less concerned that their food should be piping hot too. Many meals are cooked in the morning and kept warm on a hot plate, so that even at lunchtime they may be brought to the table lukewarm. This is the Greek way of doing things, so if you prefer to have your food hot you should choose something that has to be cooked to order, such as fish, grilled meat or a chop.

Drinks

The Greeks are not great drinkers, and their climate has never lent itself to the production of the great wines that you find in France, Spain or Italy. Nevertheless, standards are improving enormously with the demands of tourism and the increased interest in wine worldwide. Their white wines tend to be better than their reds, but many places still stock a limited range. Cheaper tavernas will almost certainly offer retsina, the resinated white wine that is unique to Greece and fairly inexpensive, whereas more up-market restaurants often no longer stock this, as it is considered unsuitable for the discerning palate. Greeks themselves are usually quite happy with a bottle of beer or a soft drink.

Hot Drinks

Nescafé has become the accepted term for an instant coffee, but if you want to try the local brew ask for a Greek coffee. In fact most people ask for a *metrio*, which is the medium-sweet version of this thick Greek brew, usually served with a glass of water. If you want your coffee sweet ask for *glikou*, or *skito* for no sugar.

Above: *octopus is enjoyed throughout the islands and is a speciality on Aígina*

Ouzo is made in many places, but Lésvos is said to produce the finest

+ 32A1

ℹ Airport Information
☎ 0735 33297; Port
Authority ☎ 0735
33280; Police/Tourist
Police ☎ 0735 31206

⛴ Daily in season from Agiá
Pelagiá, Neápoli and
Gythion on mainland, and
several weekly from
Piréas via Ýdra and
Spétses.

*The Venetian fortress of
1503, with whitewashed
churches and rugged
scenery, is typical of little-
known Kýthira*

KÝTHIRA ★★

A long way from the other Ionian islands, and a long way
from most people's travel itineraries, Kýthira sits alone off
the southern Peloponnese. In the past it has always been
considered one of the seven Ionian islands (the Greek
word for them, *Eptánissa*, literally means 'Seven Islands'),
but today it is administered from Athens and considered to
be one of the Argo-Saronic islands. However, it shares its
heritage, and in particular a past that was partly Venetian
and partly British, with the Ionians. Its isolation has kept it
from being overrun with visitors, who often like to do a
little island-hopping, and it is one of those few islands
which remain most truly Greek. There is a daily flight from
Athens, and ferries from Athens and the mainland, but the
faster hydrofoils only operate in the summer months.

Most boats arrive at the port of Kapsáli, which immediately gives a great view of the little island capital, Chóra
(Kýthira Town), which perches 275m above it. Chóra is a
quiet place, and its whitewashed houses with their vivid

blue paintwork make it one of the prettiest towns in any of the islands. Its appeal is enhanced by some of the grand old Venetian mansions which still survive, and a view out to the islet of Avgó, said to be the place where Aphrodite was born.

Around the rest of Kýthira are some good beaches, a scattering of sleepy inland villages, the remnants of Venetian castles and some small holiday resorts mostly favoured by Greek visitors.

LEFKÁDA ⭐⭐

Lefkáda, which is also sometimes called Lefkás, only just qualifies as an island because it connects to the Greek mainland by a bridge. This makes it a good base for a holiday as not only can you reach some of the other Ionian Islands from here, you could hire a car and explore parts of the lesser-visited mainland of Greece as well.

There is also plenty to explore on Lefkáda, and, while it cannot be described as the most attractive of the islands, it certainly has some wonderful natural features and unspoilt areas. The capital, Lefkáda Town, suffered badly from earthquakes in 1948 and again in 1971, and still has a makeshift feel to it. It does have several small museums, and a lively market, as well as the 17th-century Monastery of Faneroméni overlooking the town.

The main beach resorts are down the east coast, the busiest being Nydrí, while the west coast has some spectacular cliffs and is much less developed. It also has the island's best beach, the stunningly beautiful Pórto Katsíki. At the southern tip of Lefkáda is Ákra Doukáto (Cape Doukáto), also known as Lover's Leap, where the poet Sappho (▶ 14) is said to have thrown herself off the 72m-high white cliffs after being rejected by the boatman Phaon. The south-coast beach resort of Vasilikí is less developed than Nydrí, and is said to be one of the best places in the whole of Europe for windsurfing.

PAXOÍ (▶ 21, TOP TEN)

➕ 32C3
ℹ️ Port Authority ☎ 0645 22176; Tourist Police, Lefkáda Town ☎ 0645 22346; Olympic Airways in Préveza ☎ 0682 28674
🚢 Daily in season to Kefalloniá and Itháki

The south coast resort of Vaslikí on Lefkáda is a magnet for windsurfers

39

Exploring Paxoí

Distance
9km

Time
3–4 hours

Start/end point
Longós Harbour

Lunch
Vassili's (£)
✉ Waterfront, Longós
☎ 0662 31587

This walk takes you from the harbour of Longós to see some of the interior of this beautiful island, and the villages where fewer visitors venture.

From the Longós waterfront, walk to your right (as you face the sea) and follow the main road up and out of the village.

A road off to the left at the bend leads down to the town beach.

Saving the beach for later, carry on along the main road heading up and out of Longós. Even in summer the traffic is light.

The road passes by some of the quieter houses, whose colourful gardens show the Greek love of plants and flowers.

After a cluster of houses the main road swings sharply right and goes uphill for a way, before swinging back sharply left.

Don't worry – only the first half of the walk is uphill! In the village of Fontana there is a chance to stop for a drink at one of the cafés.

The fishermen's catch goes straight to the local tavernas which line the harbour at Longós on Paxoí

In Fontana take the right turning towards Magazia, only about one kilometre further on, where you reach a T-junction. If you have time, turn left at the T-junction and take the first turning on the right, down to Paxoí's impressive west-coast cliffs. If you don't want to see the cliffs, turn right at the T-junction and walk through this little hill village, and the last stretch of uphill walking.

The road takes you down past woods and olive groves, isolated farmhouses and one of the island's schools.

After a long descent you reach a proper road junction, where you turn right and right again, following the signposts back into Longós.

ZÁKYNTHOS (ZÁNTE) ⊕⊕

The Venetians regarded Zákynthos as *fiore di Levante*, the Flower of the East, and in its day the capital, Zákynthos Town, rivalled Corfu Town as the most elegant city in the Ionians. However, in 1953 came the earthquake which shattered the Ionian Islands, and Zákynthos Town was flattened. A valiant attempt was made to rebuild it in its former glory, and while it was not fully restored to its original elegance, it is still a much more pleasant place to wander round than most Greek island capitals. Above the town are the remains of the Venetian castle, which weathered the earthquake better than many of the more modern buildings, and today provides an excellent view of the bay and the town, especially at night.

The island is very popular with package-holiday tourists, particularly in the southeast corner, and nowhere more so than the sprawling resort of Laganás. Sadly the island's best beach was also the one used by loggerhead turtles for their nocturnal egg-laying, and the turtles suffered severely at the hands of developers, until more recently attempts were made to safeguard some of their nesting sites. The beach is out of bounds at night, when the turtles struggle ashore to lay their eggs, and visitors are discouraged from using beach parasols near the nesting areas, for fear of damaging eggs buried beneath the sand.

The west coast has some impressive cliffs, with the village of Kámbi the favourite spot for watching the sun sink into the Ionian at sunset. Near the northern tip of the island the Blue Caves are the major tourist attraction. Boats from the nearby little harbour of Ágios Nikólaos take visitors inside these caves, where the water is a brilliantly deep blue colour.

✚ 32C1

ℹ Tzoulati 1, Zákynthos Town ☎ 0695 27307; Airport Information ☎ 0695 28688/28322; Port Authority ☎ 0695 28117

🚢 Daily in season to Kyllíni and Pátra on mainland, and to Kefalloniá

Above: *Zákynthos Town, once destroyed by an earthquake, is a vibrant island capital once again*

DID YOU KNOW?

The motto of those who fought for Greek independence against the Turks was *ELEUTHERIA I THANATOS* (FREEDOM OR DEATH), and the nine stripes of the Greek flag are said to represent those nine syllables, though the design also owes something to the stars and stripes of the USA. The general design had been around since the independence declaration on 13 January 1822, but the flag was not officially adopted until 1833, when Otto of Bavaria became the first King of the independent Greek state.

Saronic & Northern Aegean Islands

The northern part of the Aegean is given over to several small groups of islands, which include some of the most and some of the least visited of all the Greek Islands.

The Argo-Saronic Islands (Aígina, Póros, Spétses and Ýdra) are easily reached from Athens and frequently crowded. The Sporades (Alónnisos, Skíathos, Skópelos and Skýros) are also popular with foreign holidaymakers. Lésvos is large and varied and popular with everyone. Évvoia is even larger, belongs to no island group, and remains one of the Greek Islands' secret delights.

Islands like Chíos, Ikaría and Samothráki are even less well known and appeal to visitors who want something more Greek than just lying on a beach. Sámos appeals to beach-lovers, but is large enough to have a fairly unspoilt interior and is one of the best islands for those who like walking. These islands may be hard to categorise, but they do provide something for everyone.

> ‘ *If I should die, think only this of me:*
> *That there's some corner of a foreign field*
> *That is forever England.* ’
>
> RUPERT BROOKE,
> *The Soldier* (1915)
> Rupert Brooke (1887–1915) is buried on Skýros

———————————— ● ————————————

Conifers dot the landscape of southern Évvoia, near Stýra

What to See in the Saronic and Northern Aegean Islands

✚ 28C3
ℹ Tourist Office ☎ 0297 25588; Port Authority ☎ 0297 22328
📂 Daily connections between Piréas, Aígina, Póros, Spétses and Ýdra

Naós Afaía
☎ Temple: 0297 32398
🕐 Mon–Fri 8:30–7, Sat–Sun 8:30–3
♿ Few
💵 Moderate

Above: the Temple of Aphaía on Aígina is built of local limestone

✚ 52C1
ℹ Port Authority ☎ 0424 65595; Post Office ☎ 0424 65560
📂 Daily to Skíathos, Skópelos and the mainland

AÍGINA   ✪✪

Although it is a beautiful island in the Argo-Saronic group, Aígina's proximity to Athens means that you must choose when to visit it if you want to enjoy its more relaxing side. Summer and warm weekends are out, as the ferries fill with holidaying Athenians. Who can blame them, though, when they have such an appealing destination on their doorstep? Aígina Town has a busy but attractive harbour, and the town itself some elegant 19th-century mansions surviving from the time when, briefly in 1926, Aígina Town was the first capital of a free modern Greece.

For those with an interest in even earlier history, the island also has the magnificent **Naós Afaía** (Temple of Aphaía), on the east of the island but easily reached by bus or bicycle – or even on foot as Aígina is only 8km wide – from the capital. The temple was built around 490 BC and dedicated to Aphaía, a Cretan nymph. It is one of the finest classical temple in the whole of the Greek islands.

ALÓNNISOS   ✪✪

Alónnisos is the most remote of the small Sporadic group, and the least affected by tourism. Instead it has been settled by Greeks and other Europeans who enjoy its quieter life and its scenic attractions. These attractions do not include the modern main town of Patitíri, but many settlers live up the hill in the much prettier Old Alónnisos. The rest of the island has some good beaches, while the interior ridge of hills, running the length of the island with its highest point at Mount Kouvioúli (476m, 1526ft), is ideal for walkers.

On Chíos women sort gum mastic from the island's trees

CHÍOS ⭐⭐

As yet the large island of Chíos has not been too developed for tourism, but some package-holiday groups are starting to discover the secrets that more independent travellers have known for a while: that Chíos has a lot to offer. Its industrious modern port may not seem at first sight very appealing, but it does have a good market and some interesting little museums.

The island owed part of its earlier prosperity to the many mastic trees cultivated here, producing both mastic chewing gum and the resin that was used in many domestic products such as varnishes and polishes. Now that these are mostly replaced by petroleum-based or artificial products, the mastic trees have given way to olive groves and orchards. The Mastikochoriá (Mastic Villages) such as Mestá and Pyrgí are essential visits, with their medieval and decorated houses.

➕ 47C2
ℹ️ Kanári 18, Chíos Town
☎ 0271 44389 🔵
May–Sep Mon–Fri
7–2:30, 6–9:30, Sat
10–1:30, Sun 10–12;
Oct–Apr Mon–Fri 7–2:30;
Port Authority ☎ 0271
22837/44433
🚢 Several weekly to Piréas,
Sámos and Lésvos, less
frequent services to
Límnos, Foúrni and
Pátmos

ÉVVOIA ⭐⭐

Évvoia is a law unto itself. It is the second largest Greek island after Crete, yet it is often omitted from Greek Island guidebooks because it is separated from the mainland only by the 100m-wide Évripos Channel. Guidebooks to the mainland also often exclude it because it is an island, and as a result it is too little appreciated.

Évvoia is beautifully fertile, its hills thickly wooded and separated by wide, green valleys. It has a host of attractive towns and villages, both coastal and inland. There is a good beach at Astéria, not far from the capital, Chalkída, and several good beaches at Glífa, many of which can only be reached on foot – a factor which usually deters Greek holidaymakers, who seldom stray far from their cars. Évvoia is an island which requires time to explore, not merely a hasty visit.

➕ 28C3
ℹ️ Venizélou 32, Chalkída
☎ 0221 22100; Port
Authority ☎ 0221
22236
🚢 Many daily to mainland,
and in summer to Skýros,
Skíathos, Skópelos and
Alónnisos

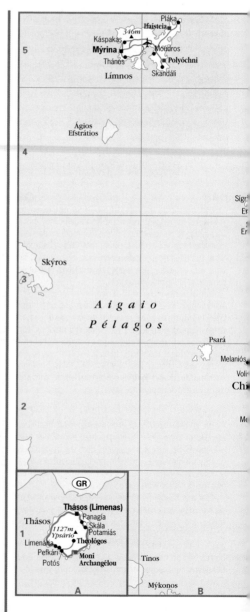

Some houses on Chíos, such as this one at Pýgri, are decorated in an elaborate Genoese style

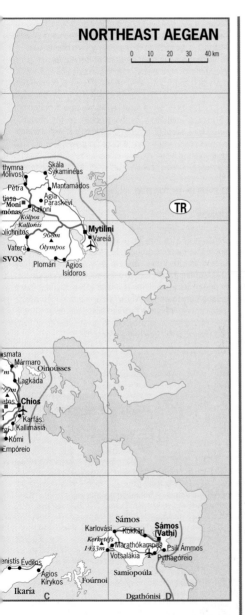

NORTHEAST AEGEAN

0   10   20   30   40 km

thymna
(Molivos)
Skála
Sykaminéas
Pétra
Mantamádos
tissa
Agía
Paraskeví
Moní
mónas
Kalloní
Kólpos
Kallonís
olichnítos
TR
Mytilíni
968m
Vareiá
Vaterá
Ólympos
SVOS
Plomári
Ágios
Isídoros

smata
Mármaro
Oinoússes
m
Lagkáda
99m
atos
Chíos
Karfás
gi
Kallimasiá
Kómi
Empóreio

Sámos
Karlovási
Kokkári
Sámos
(Vathí)
Kerketéfs
1433m
Marathókampos
Psilí Ámmos
Votsalákia
Pythagóreio
Samiopoúla
enistís Évdilos
Agios
Kírykos
Foúrnoi
Ikaría
C
Dgathónisi
D

*A family in Póros Town
enjoys the shade the high
walls bring*

47

IKARÍA ⭐⭐

For those who fear for the relentless march of tourism, a visit to Ikaría will reassure them that there are still Greek islands where the holiday industry has not yet taken hold. Indeed it has been resisted by the islanders, who have a fierce independence, and although there is a domestic airport it is too small to be used by modern charter jets.

Ikaría is not the most beautiful of the islands, but it still has some lovely scenery, including woods and orchards in the west, and frighteningly steep cliffs on both the north and south coasts. The capital is Ágios Kírykos, but even this is little more than a quiet fishing village with waterfront cafés and tavernas. The best resort on the island is Armenistís, about 60km from the capital and with a breathtaking bus journey to get there. At journey's end are two lovely sandy beaches, and inland some of the island's loveliest woodland scenery, well worth exploring on foot.

LÉSVOS (▶ 18, TOP TEN)

LÍMNOS ⭐

The closest Greek island to the entrance to Turkey's Dardanelles, Límnos has always seen a large military presence, increased at times of tension between the Greeks and the Turks. You are likely to see more Greek soldiers here than foreign tourists, but to many people that is one of its attractions. Its main town, Myrina, has a unique setting either side of a headland whose ruined 14th-century Venetian fortress splits the town in two. Myrina also has a good beach, as do the villages of Platy and Thános, both close to the capital.

A young boy on holiday goes paddling at the Akti Myrina resort complex on Límnos

PÓROS ⭐⭐

Póros is a very popular destination and a busy little island, for several reasons. Not the least of these is the fact that it's an attractive place, and is unforgettable should you first pass by it on a ferry, as boats give the illusion of sailing half-way into the town's main streets. It is very close to Athens, and just as popular with weekending Athenians as Aígina, making it not the best destination to head for in the summer if you like your peace and quiet. Finally it is a very short boat ride across the 350m-wide channel which separates it from the mainland, opening up large parts of the northern Peloponnese for further exploration – including Epidávros, Náfplio, Mykínes (Mycenae) and Tírintha (Tiryns). A short walk from the mainland port of Galatás are the lemon groves of Limonódassos, said to have more than 30,000 trees and a magnificent sight when the fruit is out.

Póros itself is in effect two separate islands, most of the one nearer the mainland (the tiny Sferiá) being taken up by the capital, Póros Town. This is a busy port but of the holiday rather than the industrial variety, and there are plenty of hotels, rooms to rent, souvenir shops and restaurants. The second island (they are in fact linked by a strip of land) is the much larger Kalávria, which is where most of the hotels are found. A circuit of the island won't take you very long, with the Monastery of Zoodóchus Pigí and the ruined Temple of Poseidon (open access) being the main sights to see.

28C2

Port Authority ☎ 0298 22274; Tourist Police (summer only) ☎ 0298 22462

Daily connections between Piréas, Aígina, Póros, Spétses and Ýdra

Above: *part of Poros Town set against the hilly interior of this small island*

DID YOU KNOW?

The Greek equivalent of 'Cheers!' when raising a glass is *yammas*, and the custom is to chink the glass of everyone else at the table. This can take some time, especially as the Greeks like to do it whenever the glasses are refilled. Always touch the top of your neighbour's glass with the top of your glass, as to use the bottom is wishing a curse on the other person.

49

The Best of Sámos

Distance
120km

Time
4–5 hours

Start/end point
Vathí

Lunch
Steve's (£)
✉ Waterfront, Karlóvasi
☎ 0273 35263

Sámos is a beautiful island and this drive explores some of its varied landscapes, making a good day out with plenty of time for stops.

Leave Vathí heading south on the coast road marked for Karlovási.

The road passes through Kokárri, where a popular holiday resort has grown up around a fishing village. It's well worth stopping for a stroll round the harbour.

Stay on the coastal road through Avlákia, with lovely sea views on your right and Sámos's hills on your left, all the way to Karlovási.

Karlovási is the island's second largest town and makes a good place to take a break, and perhaps stop for an early lunch as there is a good choice of fish restaurants here.

To continue, drive on through Karlovási, keeping left as you cross a river bed, then keep straight on for Marathokámbos (ignoring the left turn for Neó Karlovási).

The fishing port of Órmos Marathokámbou is also an increasingly popular holiday resort

As you head inland and south, you will see the Kérkis range of mountains over to your right, rising to the 1437m-height of Mt Kérkis itself.

In the village of Ágios Theódori, take the right turn marked for Marathókambos, a hill village a world away from the holiday resorts on the coast. Continue on to the beach at Órmos Marathokámbou.

Take another break by the sea, enjoying the resort's pedestrianised waterfront, with its cafés and tavernas.

Retrace your route up the winding road back to Ágios Theódori, where you turn right. Your circuit of the island continues through the hill villages of Pýrgos and Khóra (once the island's capital), heading back all the time to Vathí.

A fisherman steps ashore to the quayside of Vathí on Sámos

SÁMOS ●●●

Sámos is a mountainous and fertile island, once renowned for being the richest in the Aegean, and many of its riches today are gained by its attraction as a tourist destination. Several beach resorts have now built up but the island is so large that the interior villages are virtually untouched by overseas visitors and there are still plenty of quiet coastal places too. Its hilly, wooded landscape makes it a great destination for walkers. With its wealth of good beaches almost all round the island, it's easy to see why it has become so popular.

The capital is Vathí, also known as Sámos Town, an attractive place with a good market and elegant mansions. Its main appeal is the **Archaeological Museum** – one of the best in the Aegean – whose star exhibit is a 5m-high statue dating from 580 BC. There is another archaeological museum and some Roman remains at Pythagóreio, the island's ancient capital, while the north coast around Karlovási and Kokkári are the most developed tourist spots with good beaches.

🞧 29E3
ℹ️ Odós I Martíou, Vathí
  ☎ 0273 28530/28582;
  Port Authority, Vathí
  ☎ 0273 27318; Port
  Authority, Pythagóreio
  ☎ 0273 61225
🚢 Daily to Pátmos, Léros,
  Kálymnos and Kós,
  several weekly to Piréas,
  Chíos, Foúrni, Ikaría,
  Náxos, Páros and Sýros,
  less frequent to other
  islands

Archaeological Museum
✉️ Kapetán Gymnasiárchou
  Kateváni, Vathí
☎ 0273 27469
🕐 Tue–Sun 9–2:30
💰 Moderate

SAMOTHRÁKI ●●

Samothráki is one of the most spectacular of the Greek islands, a granite mass looming out of the Aegean, little more than 20km across and yet its highest point is the 1,611m of Mount Fengári. It also has the remains of the **Sanctuary of the Great Gods**, which was a major religious centre for almost a thousand years from about 700 BC. The site is surprisingly extensive and has yielded some splendid artefacts. The island has a few beaches but the best are only accessible by boat and it is an island for history-lovers and peace-seekers rather than sun-worshippers. Picturesque Samothráki village, tucked away among the hills in the islands interior, is medieval and the main centre of population, although still not very big,

🞧 29D4
ℹ️ Tourist Police ☎ 0551
  41203; Port Authority ☎
  0551 41305
🚢 Daily to Alexandroúpoli,
  less frequent to Kavála,
  both on the mainland

Sanctuary of the Great Gods
✉️ Palaiópoli
☎ 0551 41474
🕐 Tue–Sun 8:30–3
🍴 None
♿ None
💰 Moderate

51

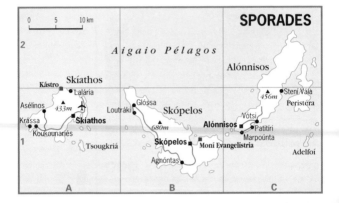

SPORADES

0   5   10 km

2

Aigaio Pélagos

Alónnisos

Kástro   Skíathos
Laláfia

Asélinos   ▲433m
Krássa   ✈ **Skíathos**
Koukounariés

Tsougkriá

Glóssa
Loutráki   Skópelos
▲680m

Skópelos

Agnóntas

▲456m   ●Stení Vála
Peristéra

Vótsi
Alónnisos■   ●Patitíri
Marpoúnta

Moní Evangelístria

Adelfoí

A   B   C

SKÍATHOS ⊕⊕

For many people Skíathos has become so overdeveloped as a tourist destination that it has lost its Greek atmosphere completely. To others it has some of the best beaches in the Aegean, great scenery as a backdrop to them, and just the kind of lively nightlife that they're looking for. Depending on the kind of holiday you want, it may be ideal or it may be a nightmare.

Life centres on Skíathos Town, which is where the ferries come in and is also close to the island's airport. It has some good eating places, and you will want to be there to sample the pubs and clubs, many of which keep going till dawn. There are said to be over sixty beaches around the island, including some that can only be reached by boat. Those on the south coast are easily reached by bus from Skíathos Town, are sheltered from the north wind and have great watersports facilities.

SKÓPELOS ⊕⊕⊕

Skópelos has much of the beauty of Skíathos but without the crowds, partly because it also lacks the numerous beaches of its neighbour. It does have its own beaches, but these are mainly pebble rather than sand, and tricky to get to by land. Some are only accessible by boat, which for many visitors is an attraction rather than a drawback. It means Skópelos has so far escaped the rampant tourist development on Skíathos. The lack of beaches is due in part to the fact that much of the island's coastline is dominated by dramatic cliffs, while the interior of the island is green and fertile, covered with olive groves, pine woods and orchards.

Skópelos Town is the focal point, and is where the boats come in – though most also stop at the little port of Loutráki in the northwest corner, which can make a good base for a quieter holiday. Skópelos Town has a lively waterfront, lined with the usual array of bars, cafés, tavernas and souvenir shops, while the winding streets behind, leading up to the ruins of a Venetian castle, provide the archetypal Greek island scenes of whitewashed houses, tiled roofs, blue doors and windows, and little balconies. Skópelos Town also has one of the few sandy beaches on the island.

The second largest town is Glóssa, perched high above the little port of Loutráki, and much more Greek in feel. There are a number of typical old *kafeneons* where the men gather to put the world to rights over cups of Greek coffee.

✚ 52B1

🛈 Tourist Police, Papadiamántis ☎ 0427 23172 🕐 Daily 8AM–9PM; Port Authority ☎ 0427 22216/22017; Police ☎ 0427 21111; Post Office ✉ Papadiamántis/Evangelístra ☎ 0427 22011 🕐 Mon–Fri 7:30–2

🚢 Daily to Skópelos, Alónnisos and the mainland

✚ 52A1

🛈 Port Authority ☎ 0424 22180; Tourist Police (Skópelos Town) ☎ 0424 22235; Tourist Police (Glóssa) ☎ 0424 33333

🚢 Daily to Skíathos, Alónnisos and the mainland

Left: *this church in Skíathos Town, with its roof of red tiles, is typical of the Northern Aegean Islands*

53

DID YOU KNOW?

The word icon comes from the Greek, *eikenai*, meaning to be like. Icons are not solely images of saints or other holy people, but can also depict religious events. In the 8th century the Iconoclastic Movement began, whose members believed icons to be idols, and worship of them to be idolatry, and therefore forbidden. This movement lasted into the next century, but when it died out icons took on the rather formal look that we recognise today.

🔴 29D3
ℹ️ Skýros Town ☎ 0222 93789 🕐 Daily 7:30–2:30, Jul–Aug 9–3, 6:30–11; Police ☎ 0222 91274; Port Authority ☎ 0222 96475
🚢 Daily to Kými on Évvoia

Laskarína Bouboulína is commemorated with a statue at Dapia, on Spétses

---

🔴 28C2
ℹ️ Port Authority ☎ 0298 72245; Tourist Police ☎ 0298 73744
🚢 Daily connections between Piréas, Aígina, Póros, Spétses and Ýdra

SKÝROS ✪✪

Skýros is an unusual and bewitching island in the shape of a butterfly, and locals insist that the two 'wings' were once two separate islands. The north has gentle, green rolling hills, covered in places in pine forests, while the south is barren and mountainous, and sparsely populated. It is at the southern end that the British poet Rupert Brooke is buried. There is a statue dedicated to 'Immortal Poetry' in Skýros Town, the island capital. Its white cubic houses cluster below the remains of a Byzantine fortress. Skýros is starting to attract visitors in increasing numbers, but it is still very unspoilt – witness the continued survival of the traditional Skýros Goat Dance, which takes place during the pre-Lenten Carnival.

SPÉTSES ✪✪

Spétses is the furthest from Athens of all the Argo-Saronic Islands, tucked away around a prong of the Peloponnese, but it is only marginally less busy than the others. It gets its share of day-trippers during the summer, and on warm weekends all year round, yet although it is fairly small it is big enough to provide escape from the crowds. The centre is covered with pine forests, and around the coast there are plenty of quiet beaches, as well as busier ones.

Spétses Town, the only major settlement, is a harbour town that manages to combine elegance with the bustle of the modern tourist trade. It has a couple of small museums, a cathedral and a statue to the local heroine, Laskarína Bouboulína, who, in 1821, led the island's uprising against the Turks.

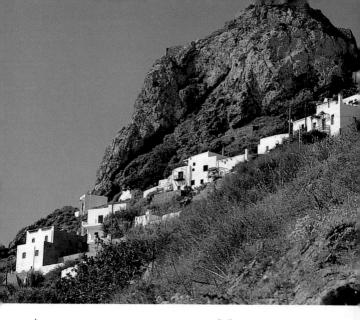

THÁSOS ★★

Standing alone just 12km off the coast of Greece's province of Makedonía, Thásos is understandably popular with visitors from both Greece and overseas. It is far from overrun, however, and local life carries on alongside tourism. It is a fertile island that is not reliant on tourism, and has olive groves and orchards, and is especially noted for the quality of its honey and walnuts. The latter can be bought everywhere, made into a thick treacle-like jam, preserved or sold as unusual sweets.

The centre of the island is hilly and wooded, although forest fires affected large parts of it several years ago and it is only just starting to recover. The highest point is Mount Ipsárion which is 1,204m high and can be walked, but you will need a good map, good boots and plenty of time.

The main town is Thásos Town, also known as Limenás, which is an attractive and busy little port, in a fine setting surrounded by pine-covered hills. Ancient Thásos has some good Roman and Greek remains, including the Agorá and Theatre, and the remnants of a fort that dates back to the 5th century BC.

A coast road circles the island, linking the many villages and beach resorts, large and small. You can stop off almost anywhere and be sure of finding somewhere to stay, and a beach to lie on. Limenária is the second largest town, but not the most attractive. Nearby Potós is better, a busy resort with a wonderful kilometre-long stretch of beach.

YDRA (► 26, TOP TEN),

✚ 29D5
ℹ Port Authority ☎ 0593 22106; Tourist Police ☎ 0593 23111; Police ☎ 0593 22500
✉ Daily to Kavála on the mainland

Ancient Thásos (Agorá, Theatre, Archaeological Museum)
☎ 0593 22180
⏲ Ruins: Daily during daylight hours; Museum: Tue–Fri 8–7, Sat–Sun 8:30–3

Above: *the outcrop above Skýros Town, from where the mythical Athenian hero Theseus is said to have been pushed to his death*

Cyclades

Ask most people what their image of the Greek Islands is, even if they have never been there, and chances are it will be an image of the Cyclades. Here you find cubic architecture in abundance: whitewashed houses, vivid blue doors and windows, blue-domed churches and all beneath a sky of deepest aquamarine.

This is the Cyclades, the largest island group, which gets its name from the fact that the islands lie more or less in a circle around Dílos (Delos), which was one of the most sacred places in Ancient Greece. Today Tínos is a place of special pilgrimage in these islands. Being such a large group the islands offer plenty of variety, ranging from hedonistic places like Mýkonos and Íos, the busy and rather different volcanic island of Thíra (Santoríni), through to lesser-known islands such as Anáfi, Kímolos and Síkinos.

> *The isles of Greece, the isles of Greece!*
> *Where burning Sappho loved and sung.*
> *Where grew the arts of war and peace,*
> *Where Delos rose, and Phoebus sprung!*
> *Eternal summer gilds them yet,*
> *But all, except their sun, is set.*

LORD BYRON (1788–1824)
from his poem *Don Juan*

———————————•———————————

A small church on Sérifos, typical of the Cycladic style

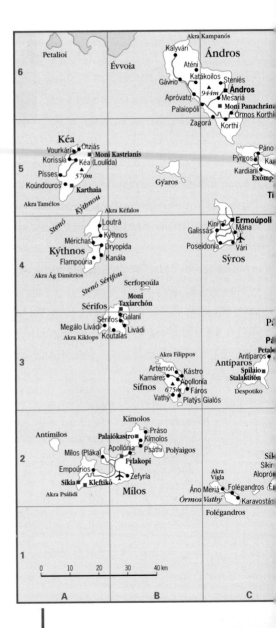

CYCLADES

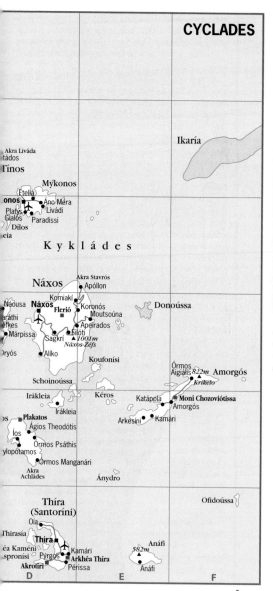

Ikaría

Akra Liváda
tádos
Tínos
Mýkonos
Etelía
onos Áno Méra
Platýs Livádi
Gialós Paradíssi
Dilos
eia

Kykládes

Náxos
Akra Stavrós
Apóllon
Náousa Náxos Komiakí
aráthi Flerió Koronós
éfkes Moutsoúna
Márpissa Apeírados
Sagkrí Filóti
Dryós Alíko ▲1001m
Náxos-Zéfs
Koufonísi

Donoússa

Schoinoússa

Kéros

Iráklia
Iráklia

Órmos
Aigialís 822m Amorgós
Kríkelo

Katápola Moní Chozoviótissa
Amorgós
Arkesíni Kamári

os Plakatos
Ágios Theodótis
íos
Órmos Psáthis
ylopótamos
Órmos Manganári
Akra
Achládes
Ánydro

Thíra
(Santoríni)
Oía
Thirasía
Thíra
éa Kaméni Kamári
spronísi Pyrgos 582m Anáfi
Akrotíri Arkhéa Thíra
Périssa Anáfi

Ofidoússa

D E F

A monk from the Panachrandou Monastery on Ándros

What to See in the Cyclades

AMORGÓS ✪✪✪

Amorgós is only a slim little island but manages to pack in a lot of dramatic mountain scenery, making it an ideal island for walkers. For a long time it was very much 'off the beaten track', known only to a few aficionados, but in recent years visitors have been arriving in ever-increasing numbers. It is still far from being overly commercialised, but you certainly won't be alone here in high summer.

There is only one sandy beach, but plenty of other good ones if you don't mind lying on pebbles. The capital is Amorgós Town, or Chóra, where white houses gather around the remains of a 13th-century Venetian fortress. The town is said to have over forty chapels and churches, one of which claims to be the smallest in Greece. This may well be true, as Ágios Fanoúrios has room inside it for just three people.

ANÁFI ✪

If you want to get away from it all, then Anáfi will certainly allow you to do that. It is only a 90-minute ferry ride away from Thíra, but a world away in terms of the numbers of tourists it attracts. In the main town of Chóra there are only a handful of rooms to rent, a few cafés, some tavernas to eat in and just the basic tourist facilities: bakery, post office, telephone office. Along the south coast of the rather bleak, rocky island is a string of inviting beaches, the best being at Roúkounas, and these are what attract the few summer visitors.

ÁNDROS ✪✪

The second-largest island in the Cyclades, Ándros has been a favourite with Athenian and other Greek holidaymakers for a long time, but overseas visitors have only more recently started to discover it. And there is a lot to discover. It is a lush island, about 35km from one end to the other, with dry-stone walls an unusual feature of the landscape, a legacy of the Venetians. Another is the many tall, white dovecotes to be seen.

59F3

Tourist Information (Jeyzed Travel) ☎ 0286 61253; Port Authority ☎ 0286 61216

Three weekly to Piréas, Thíra, Íos, Náxos and Páros, less frequent to other Cycladic islands and to Astypálaia

---

59E1

Tourist Information ☎ 0285 71278; Port Authority ☎ 0285 71259; Police ☎ 0285 71210

Several weekly to Náxos, Páros, Rafína (for Athens), Sýros, Tínos and Mýkonos, less frequent to other islands.

58C6

Port Authority ☎ 0282 22250; Police ☎ 0282 22300

Daily to Rafína (for Athens), Tínos and Mýkonos, several weekly to Sýros, less frequent to some other Cycladic islands

---

The Archaeological Museum on Ándros has some fine local finds, such as this graceful statue of Hermes

DID YOU KNOW?

The Mediterranean monk seal has been around for 15 million years, but today it is Europe's most endangered mammal with only 400 left in the Mediterranean. Its relative, the Caribbean monk seal, became extinct in the 1950s. The Mediterranean monk seal is, as its name suggests, a retiring creature, and is also easily disturbed and affected by pollution.

Ándros Town, or Chóra, is a beautifully elegant place of grand mansions, quiet squares and a marble-paved main street that has been pedestrianised. A bridge leads to a small island on which are the remnants of a 13th-century Venetian castle, while the **Archaeological Museum** is also one of the best in the Cyclades. A rarity is the **Museum of Modern Art**, which has work by Picasso and Braque alongside modern Greek artists, the reason being that it was founded by the wealthy Goulandris ship-owning family, who have long been patrons of the arts around the world and who originally came from Ándros.

The rest of the island is perfect for exploring on foot – which is just as well as the bus service is limited. The village of Messariá is not far from Chóra, and should be on everyone's itinerary regardless of how you get there. It is a beautiful medieval village, with a 12th-century Byzantine church and the ruins of old tower houses still to be seen.

Archaeological Museum
⊠ Plateía Kairi
🕐 Tue–Sun 8:30–3
✋ Moderate

Museum of Modern Art
⊠ Plateía Kairi
🕐 Wed–Sun 10–2, also 6–8 in summer
✋ Expensive

The red-roofed village of Stenies is closed to traffic and said to be the finest on Ándros

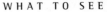

59D4
Only served by day-trip boats from Mýkonos

Archaeological Museum
☎ 0289 22259
🍴 Café (££)
🕐 Tue–Sun 8:30–3
♿ None
💷 Expensive

DÍLOS (DELOS)   ⭐⭐⭐

The Lion Terrace on the sacred island of Delos must be one of the most photographed sights in Greece after the Parthenon. Made of white marble, these beasts make a magnificent image beneath the deep blue Cycladic skies. The image would have been even more stunning before three of the original lions were removed and taken to Venice. In 1999 the remaining lions were taken into the Archaeological Museum for safe-keeping and replaced with replicas. The lions were carved in about the 7th or 6th centuries bc, by which time the island was already a major sacred site. Its origins go back to 1000 bc when the Ionians arrived here and established it as a place for the worship of Apollo. They founded the Delian Games, an annual festival of sport and arts held in Apollo's honour. From this, Delos developed not merely into the holiest site in the islands but also a flourishing town and port.

In addition to the Lion Terrace, highlights of the archaeological site today include the House of Dionysos, inside which is a wonderfully preserved mosaic, the Theatre, which held 5,500 people, and the House of the Dolphins, containing a beautifully detailed 2nd-century bc mosaic depicting two dolphins. The Archaeological Museum displays the remaining lions and other finds from the site.

Delos has fine mosaics as well as monuments, this depicting a panther on the floor of the House of Masks

Day-trippers to the island arrive by boat from Mýkonos (► 19) and usually stay for about three hours, as boats leave Mýkonos at about 8:30 or 9 each morning in summer, and return again at about 1 or 1:30PM (there are fewer trips in winter). The crossing takes about 40 minutes, and it is also possible to pre-book a guided tour if you wish.

58C2
ℹ Tourist Information (Sottovento Agency)
☎ 0286 41430
🚢 Several weekly to Piréas, Kýthnos, Sérifos, Sífnos, Milos and Síkinos, less frequent to other islands

FOLÉGANDROS   ⭐

This tiny island, about 14km long, is shielded by dramatic cliffs that rise up to 300m above the sea. It is one of the few places where the growing of barley – a staple crop in the Cyclades – still takes precedence over the cultivation of tourism. That is changing, however, as visitors discover the unspoilt charms that lie behind those cliffs, and the traffic-free centre of Folégandros Town, the capital.

ÍOS ✪

Íos has beaches and bars, and lots of them. Íos Town (Chóra) is where all the action is, and is not the place to be if you like early nights. The local authorities have been trying to discourage some of the rowdier behaviour by closing bars and clubs earlier on weekdays (earlier being 3AM), but it remains an island for party animals unless you visit out of season. Then you might enjoy the capital's village atmosphere, or a visit to Plakatos, where Homer is reputed to be buried.

 59D2

✉ Harbour at Gialós
☎ 0286 91028
🕐 Opens when ferries come in; Port Authority
☎ 0286 91264
🚢 Daily to Piréas, Páros, Náxos and Thíra, several weekly to Síkinos, Folégandros and Crete

KÉA ✪✪

Kéa is the closest of the Cycladic islands to Athens, making it a popular starting point for island-hoppers, and a weekend retreat for Athenians. The busiest resorts are Korissía (the island's port) and nearby Vourkári, but it is easy to get to quieter places such as Písses and Otziás. The capital, Kéa Town (also called Loulís, Loulída and Chóra), is set up in the hills around a 13th-century Venetian castle. It is noted for its 26 windmills on the Mountain of the Mills, its winding back streets and its distinctive red-roofed houses.

58A5

ℹ Port Authority ☎ 0288 21344; Tourist Police ☎ 0288 21100
🚢 Daily to Lávrio (for Athens), two weekly to Kýthnos

Above: *the windmills on Kéa indicate its rural nature, despite its proximity to Athens*

KÍMOLOS ★★

The population of Kímolos is less than 1,000, and even in midsummer this does not increase much as there is only accommodation for about 100 visitors. With good beaches and a scattering of little communities, it makes a great base for those who want a relaxing time on an unspoilt Greek island. Kímolos Town, or Chóra, is a delightful hill village of whitewashed houses and winding lanes. It overlooks several windmills (the last working mills in the Cyclades), and is overlooked in turn by a Venetian castle.

KÝTHNOS (THERMÍA) ★

The local name of Thermía comes from the thermal springs at Loutrá, which bring the majority of Greek visitors to soak in their beneficial waters. Most of these come in midsummer, and relatively few foreigners bother to include Kýthnos on their itineraries, even though there are daily connections with Athens and with Mílos. Those who do, find a low-key lifestyle where farming and fishing still predominate.

MÍLOS ★

Mílos has an incredibly varied landscape, with hot springs and weird rock formations indicating its origins as a volcanic island. It has been left with a heritage of rich minerals, and the drawback is that the interior is scarred in places by quarries. On the plus side are a string of good, sandy beaches and some pretty fishing villages. Mílos is known to the world as the place where the statue of the Venus de Milo was found in 1820, and a sign marks the spot amid the ruins of ancient Melos.

MÝKONOS (► 19, TOP TEN)

Left: *boat houses at Klima on Milos*
Below: *one of Náxos's many medieval churches*

NÁXOS ●●●

Lots of superlatives apply to Náxos. It is the biggest island in the Cyclades, and the most mountainous. In Mount Zas (or Zeus) at 1,004m it has the highest point in the Cyclades. It is the most fertile of these islands, and the only one which could be self-sufficient. It also has a wealth of historical remains, having been first settled about 5,000 years ago. Add to this some brilliant beaches, picturesque fishing harbours and rugged mountain towns and villages, and you have an island which seems to have everything. One thing it doesn't have, to the extent you might expect, is tourists. Certainly there are plenty in high summer, but thanks to the size of the island (about 25km x 35km at its widest) the visitors disperse readily. It is starting to change, though, and its recently opened airport now brings in charter jets from Europe, so some resorts will inevitably be transformed.

🞧 59D3
ℹ️ Harbour, Náxos Town
☎ 0285 24358/25201; Port Authority ☎ 0285 22300; Tourist Police ☎ 0285 22100; Airport ☎ 0285 23292
🚢 Daily to Piréas, Páros, Íos, Sýros and Thíra, several weekly to Amorgós, Crete, Tínos, Síkinos, Folégandros, Ándros, Anáfi, Rhodes, Ikaría and Sámos

Náxos Town, or Chóra, is busy but still a relaxed place to visit, with the old part clustered around the impressive remains of its 13th-century Venetian castle. Down on the waterfront are the inevitable cafés, bars and fish tavernas. Filóti is the town to head for if you want to tackle the walk to the top of Mount Zas, which is easily done in a few hours and gives unrivalled views over the island and the Aegean. Take a map or a local guidebook for walkers. The prettiest village on Náxos is undoubtedly nearby Apeírados, with its marbled streets and – rare for the Cyclades – unwhite-washed houses.

Above: *café life by the
harbour at Parikiá on
Páros*

PÁROS ●●●

Páros has long been a wealthy island, thanks to the high-quality translucent marble that was mined here and much-valued by the sculptors and architects of Ancient Greece: the Venus de Milo was made from Parian marble. It is also a beautifully fertile island, rich in orchards, lemon groves, vineyards and fields of grain. It has a great deal of typically Cycladic architecture, beautiful unspoilt villages, and many perfect beaches, so it is little surprise that it is a popular destination for holidaymakers.

It is a long way from being over-run, however, as the island is big enough to cope with the tens of thousands of visitors who arrive in the summer, and also has its own strong character still very much to the fore. Páros Town, or Parikiá, combines being a busy port with a lively water-front, and a traditional Greek town with its narrow back streets. The oldest part is around the Venetian castle, built in the 13th century, partly using white marble from old Greek temples to build its thick walls.

Parian marble was also used in the 10th century to rebuild the unusual Cathedral of Panagía Ekatondapilianí, or Our Lady of the Hundred Doors, referring to the number it is said to contain. Another story claims that there are 99 and when the 100th is discovered then Constantinople (Istanbul) will be returned to Greece. The present church dates back to the 6th century, when it was built by the Emperor Justinian, though the first building on this site was originally put up in the 4th century, by the Emperor Constantine at the instigation of his daughter Helen, later St Helen. She was journeying from Rome to the Holy Land in search of the True Cross when her ship was forced to seek shelter from a storm in Páros. She vowed that if her quest was successful, which it allegedly was, she would build a church on this island.

The **Archaeological Museum** is also worth visiting, in order to learn more about the history of the island and its marble in particular. There are some finds from the Temple of Apollo, whose remains can be seen to the north-east of the town, and a statue of the Winged Nike from the 5th century BC. The prize exhibit is part of the 'Parian Chronicles', a history of Greece up until 264 BC carved on marble, the rest being in the Ashmolean Museum in Oxford, England.

More marble, in the streets this time, is in the hill town of Léfkes, one of the loveliest on the island and its medieval capital. The quarries themselves are close by at Maráthi, and still being worked. The best beaches on Páros are on the north, around Náousa. This is the island's second port, the inevitable fishing village that was discovered by visitors, to such an extent that in 1997 the Greek Government made it the first place in the country where there was a restriction on endless development. As a result, it has not been totally swamped and the pretty harbour can still be enjoyed. If you are there on 23 August you can enjoy the islanders re-enacting a battle they had with Barbarossa, the pirate.

Archaeological Museum
- ✉ Behind Panagía
  Ekatondapilianí
- ☎ 0284 21231
- 🕐 Tue-Sun 8:30-2:30
- 💰 Cheap

The 11th-century Cathedral of Our Lady of the Hundred Doors

SÉRIFOS ✪

Sérifos is a small island where seemingly not much has happened over the years – not even much tourism. Its very name, 'the barren one', does not inspire, and nor does the knowledge that it has been heavily mined for iron and copper. And yet, increasing numbers of people are making their way there, and it does have some good, sandy beaches and is excellent terrain for walking. Boats arrive at the pretty and unpretentious little port of Livádi, which has a decent beach and basic tourist amenities, with other good beaches a short walk away. From the port there is a stunning view of the main town, Chóra or Sérifos Town, straddling a rock up above, with the ruins of a Venetian fortress behind, on top of which sits a tiny and dazzling white church.

58B3

Port Authority ☎ 0281 51470; Police ☎ 0281 51300

Daily to Piréas, Sífnos and Milos. Several weekly to Kímolos, Folégandros, Sýkinos, Íos and Thíra, less frequently to other Cycladic and Dodecanesian islands and Crete

SÍFNOS ✪✪

Chapels and churches, windmills and dovecotes, orchards, vineyards and olive groves – all fill the landscape of Sífnos, which has always been more popular with Greeks than with overseas visitors, mainly because they hardly knew about it. Now that they do they are coming here in ever-increasing numbers, vastly outnumbering the 2,000 residents in midsummer. That is not to say that the island has been spoilt, far from it: it has sandy beaches, lots of tracks and trails for walkers, and some beautiful villages. One of these is Kástro, the ancient and medieval capital which overlooks the sea on the east coast. The present capital is Apollónia, a typical tiny Cycladic town where the whitewashed walls contrast with blue painted doors and pink bougainvillaea. To add to its appeal, Sífnos is said to produce the best chefs in the whole of Greece.

58B3

Quayside, Kamáres ☎ 0284 31977 ⏰ opens to coincide with ferries; Port Authority ☎ 0284 31617

Daily to Piréas, Sérifos and Milos, several weekly to Kímolos, Folégandros, Síkinos, Íos and Thíra, less frequently to other Cycladic and Dodecanesian islands, and Crete

The hill village of Kástro is on the east coast of Sífnos

SÍKINOS ⊘

For those who think Folégandros (► 63) is too busy (and by comparison to most islands it's a backwater), Síkonos should provide the remedy. There are a few basic amenities down at the harbour of Aloprónoia (a beach, a few tavernas, some rooms to rent), from where a bus or a steep hike takes you up to Síkinos Town, or Kástro-Chóra. This is two villages rolled into one, with some 18th-century houses clustered protectively inside the walls of the fortress, or *kastro*, and the rest of the town outside. There is not a great deal to do other than perhaps walk to the island's few notable features. These include the ruined 18th-century Monastery of Zoödóchou Pigís, the scant Roman remains at Episkopí or to one of the beaches: Ágios Pandelímonas is the best, on the opposite side of the island from Síkinos Town.

SÝROS ⊘⊘

Although it is the administrative capital of the Cyclades, Sýros itself sees very few foreign tourists. The fact that it is fairly barren and rocky accounts partly for this, but if you were to call in on one of the many ferries that use the port of Ermoúpolis, you would never think that this is as far as many visitors get. Ermoúpolis blends into the other two areas of the main town, Áno Sýros and Vrondádo, which have traditionally been Catholic and Orthodox respectively. Each has many churches and back streets to explore, while the main resort is at Poseidonía in the southwest corner. There are many other small resorts and hill villages to find, and though it may be barren you will be left wondering why more people don't enjoy its unspoilt delights – or indeed the island speciality of *loukoúmia*: Greek Delight here, Turkish Delight elsewhere in the world.

THÍRA (► 24, TOP TEN)

✚ 58C2
ℹ Port Authority ☎ 0286 51222
🚢 Several weekly to Piréas, Folégandros, Kýthnos, Sérifos, Sifnos and Milos, less frequent to some other Cycladic islands

Above: the smaller the island, the warmer the welcome, and the more curious the children will be, as here on Síkinos

✚ 58C4
ℹ Dodekanésou ☎ 0281 86725; Police ✉ Platía Miaoúli, Ermoúpolis ☎ 0281 82620; Airport ☎ 0281 22255; Port Authority ☎ 0281 82633
🚢 Daily to Piréas, Tinos, Mýkonos, Náxos and Páros, less frequently to other Cycladic and Dodecanesian islands

Exploring Thíra

Distance
50km

Time
6 hours (with long stops)

Start/end point
Thíra

Lunch
The Boathouse (££)
✉ Kamári Beach
☎ 0286 32474

This is not a long drive, but allow plenty of time because of the winding roads and the views.

Leave Thíra driving southeast, following the signs for the airport, but ignore the left turn to the airport and continue straight on towards Akrotíri. Beyond the village of Megalochóri, look for the right turn for the Boutari vineyard. You can divert here if you wish, to see one of the most famous wineries in Greece, but return to the main road to continue. Look out for the right–hand turn to Akrotíri, a few kilometres after the vineyard.

The views along here of Thíra's Caldera are wonderful, and you are sure to want to stop for photographs.

In the village of Akrotíri, follow the signs for Ancient Akrotíri.

The well-preserved Minoan city of Ancient Akrotíri is one of the finest archaeological sites in the Cyclades.

Drive back through the village of Akrotíri, then Megalochóri, and take the right turn to Pýrgos.

The three-storeyed belfry in Pýrgos, the oldest surviving village on Thíra

Pýrgos is one of the island's oldest and prettiest villages, from where you can drive up to Profítis Ilías, the island's highest point (566m), with its 18th-century monastery.

From Pýrgos drive on to Kamári Beach, a good place for lunch. Retrace your route through Pýrgos and turn right at the main road back through Thíra Town. At the far end take a left turn to Imerovígli.

This coast road gives wonderful views out to sea.

On rejoining the main road turn left and follow the road to Oía, stunningly situated on the end of the island, before returning to Thíra.

The Megalochóri ('Great Grace'), the holy icon on Tínos, in the Church of the Panagía Evangelístra

TÍNOS ✪✪✪

Tínos is known as the island that almost sinks beneath the weight of pilgrims who visit the icon at the **Church of Panagía Evangelístra**. On 25 March and 15 August, especially, sick people come from all over Greece hoping for a cure from the icon, which was found by a nun in 1823 and is believed to have miraculous powers. The yellow church of the Panagía is in the port and capital, Tínos Town, on the south coast. It is full of small museums and galleries, as a great deal of work has been sent to the church and put on display, and there is an **Archaeological Museum** too.

Tínos has some lovely, rolling, fertile countryside, liberally dotted with distinctive white dovecotes – there are said to be 800 of them across the island, a legacy from Venetian rule – and over 1,200 chapels. With its good sandy beaches and network of roads and tracks, it makes a great base for those who like walking. The highest point on the island is Tsiknías at 729m, and there is also the peak of Exómpourgo, at 640m. Both make good targets for walks, giving lovely views of the Tínos landscape and its many unspoilt hill villages. If you are interested in arts and crafts then Pýrgos is a village renowned for the fine marble sculpting that it produces – workshops can be visited – and Tínos itself is known for its green marble, mined at Marlás.

✚ 58C5

🛈 Port Authority ☎ 0283 22220; Tourist Police ☎ 0283 22255

🚢 Daily to Piréas, Ándros, Sýros and Mýkonos, several weekly to Páros, Náxos, Thíra, Skíathos, Crete, Thessaloníki and Amorgós. Less frequent to other Cycladic and Dodecanesian islands

Church of Panagía Evangelístra
🖂 Megalochóri
☎ 0283 22756
🕐 Daily 8–8
🎟 Free

Archaeological Museum
🖂 Megalochóri
☎ 0283 22670
🕐 Tue–Sun 8:30–3
🎟 Moderate

Dodecanese

This is the most southerly group of Greek islands, and only Crete lies closer to Africa. In summer the temperatures can soar, which is what brings the sun-worshippers flocking to their sand and shingle beaches. Sunshine is guaranteed, and in some islands water shortages can occur. In spring the islands are green from winter rain, but by the time autumn comes around they have been burnt as brown as any sunbather.

The islands string out along the coast of Turkey, and only became part of Greece in 1948. They range from the big package-holiday destinations such as Kós and Rhodes to tiny specks like Kastellórizo, which is closer to Turkey than it is to any other Greek island. The Dodecanese also contain gems like Sými, arguably one of the most beautiful of all Greek islands, the holy island of Pátmos, and islands where tourism has not yet swamped the local culture, like Tílos and Léros.

> *'Little islands out at sea, on the horizon*
> *keep suddenly showing a whiteness, a*
> *flash and a furl, a hail*
> *of something coming, ships a-sail from*
> *over the rim of the sea.'*

D H LAWRENCE (1885–1930),
from *The Greeks are Coming*

———————•———————

This immaculate church is in Apéri, former capital of Kárpathos

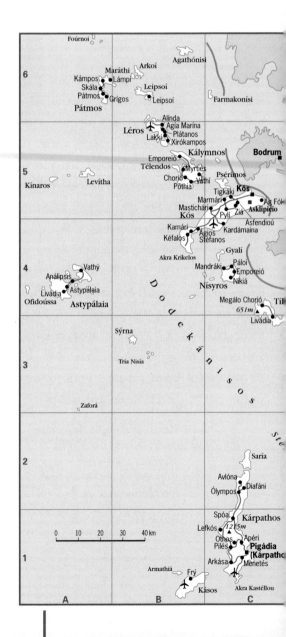

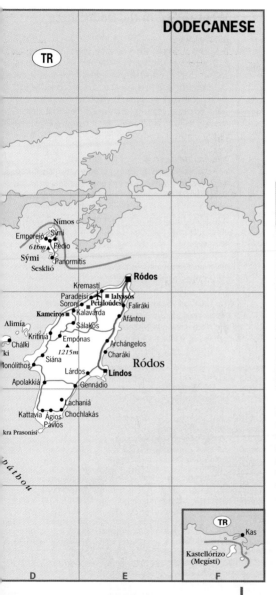

DODECANESE

TR

Nímos
Emporeió ● ● Sými
6 t6m ▲ ● Pédio
Sými ● Panormítis
Sesklió

■ **Ródos**

Kremastí
Paradeísi ● ● ■ **Ialyssós**
Soroní ● **Petaloúdes** ● Faliráki
Kámeiros ■ ● Kalavárda
Sálakos ● Afántou
Alimía
Kritiniá ● Empónas
Chálki ▲ 1215m ● Archángelos
ki ● Siána ● Charáki
Monólithos **Ródos**
Lárdos ● ■ **Líndos**
Apolakkiá ● ● Gennádio

Lachaniá
Kattaviá ● ● Chochlakás
Ágios ● Pávlos
kra Prasonísi

θάτθου

TR
● Kas
Kastellórizo
(Megísti)

D   E   F

Mosaic outside
the Kastellania
Palace, from 1507,
in Plateía
Ippokratous, in the
Old Town of
Rhodes

What to See in the Dodecanese

ASTYPÁLAIA ✪✪

Astypálaia is shaped like a butterfly, which is appropriate as it appears to be fluttering away from the Dodecanese with which it is grouped for administrative purposes, to the Cyclades with which it is probably more at home. The two 'wings' of the island are joined by an isthmus which is only 100m across at its narrowest. Among the island's distinguishing features are the fact that it has no snakes, and among Greeks it is renowned for its honey and both the quantity and quality of its fish – and there are plenty of good fish tavernas in which to test the claim.

Astypálaia Town, or Chóra, clusters round a hilltop fortress, now in ruins, the white buildings spilling down the slopes and joining up with the harbour area, known as Gialós. It has become a firm favourite with many travellers, who enjoy its harbour, its beach and its mix of building styles: Italianate mansions, Cycladic white cubes, Turkish balconies.

The island's unusual shape means that it has more coastline per square metre than most, with some long jagged inlets, quiet sheltered coves and a number of good beaches such as Tzanáki, near the capital, or at Análipsis and Sténo as you cross the isthmus towards the eastern 'wing'. Análipsis is the second largest town on the island, and is also known as Maltezána, but there is precious little here save a few tavernas, a beach and an increasing number of holiday villas.

➕ 74A4
ℹ In the windmill in Chóra/booth on quayside
☎ 0243 61412 Ⓖ
Open to meet ferries, otherwise Jun–Sep daily, hours vary; Port Authority
☎ 0243 61208; Airport
☎ 0243 61665; Police
☎ 0243 61207
⛴ Several weekly to Amórgos, Náxos, Páros, Piréas and Sýros, less frequent to some other Dodecanesian islands

Low archways in the fortress above the town of Astypálaia

CHÁLKI ★★

With its tiny population, Chálki is one of the quieter islands, except in midsummer when it bursts into life as a holiday destination. This is thanks in no small way to the efforts of a British holiday company, Laskarina, which has invested money in helping renovate some of the island's elegant but crumbling houses, turning them into holiday accommodation. This is more important than might first appear, as before this Chálki was in danger of losing its population completely. The sponge-fishing industry on which the islanders relied came to a halt in the early twentieth century, when their sponge fields died through disease, and slowly the inhabitants drifted away to Rhodes, Australia or America. The boosting of small-scale tourism has been the saving of the island.

The name of the island means 'copper', as this used to be mined here, another source of income that dried up. Today tourism means a growing market for the fishermen and farmers too, and Chálki is a place where visitors quickly feel part of the local family – there are still only about 300 people permanently resident, compared with 3,000 a century ago. Almost everyone lives in little Chálki Town, or Emporeió, with a large harbour where fishermen mend their nets during the day, and holiday-makers and locals spill into the handful of cafés and tavernas at night. West of Emporeió, along the wonderfully named 'Boulevard Tarpon Springs'

Greece is famous for its fresh seafood, even if not everything might appear on the menus back home

(funded by former islanders who settled in Florida), there are some quiet bays and beaches, a ruined fortress and, eventually, the deserted village of Chorió, though even here a few holiday homes have now been renovated. So far Chálki seems a model for the good that controlled tourist development can do.

+ 75D3

i Tourist Information (Chálki Tours) ☎ 0241 45281; Port Authority ☎ 0241 45220; Police ☎ 0241 45213

⌨ Daily to Rhodes, a few weekly to Crete and to a few Cycladic and other Dodecanesian islands

---

DID YOU KNOW?

Seafood can never taste better than when caught and served up on the same day. Some tavernas, however, serve up frozen fish and claim that it's fresh, which is forbidden by law. The squid season, for example, does not start until about October, so if you are offered 'fresh squid' in summer it means it was fresh when it was caught ... probably in South America.

🕂 74B5
🛈 Waterfront, Póthia
☎ 0243 29310
🕐 Apr–Oct Mon–Fri
7–2:30; Port Authority
☎ 0243 24444
🛳 Daily to Rhodes, Sámos,
Léros, Pátmos, Kós and
Piréas, less frequent to
other Dodecanesian and
Cycladic islands, seasonal
daily excursions to
Psérimos

KÁLYMNOS ✪✪

Of the islands in the Dodecanese that made a living from sponge-fishing – Sými and Chálki were others – Kálymnos was the one which became famed throughout Greece for the quality of its sponges, and its association with sponge-fishing. It is a tradition which just about clings on, as, like everywhere else, they were affected by the virus which destroyed the local sponge fields, and now just a few boats trawl further afield, to the sponging areas of Italy and off the North African coast.

You will still see thousands of sponges for sale in the main town of Póthia, a very busy and not very attractive port, but these are mostly imported in order to at least keep the sponge-selling trade alive. With a recent increase in tourism, the market for these sponges continues. The main tourist development has taken place on the west coast of the island, resulting in a string of pleasant resorts such as Mirtiés and Massoúri, with good beaches and a splendid view across to the hilly little island of Télendos across the bay.

On the east coast, the small port of Ría, also called Vathí, makes a good base for those who like walking more than sunbathing. The Vathí valley which runs inland from here is green with orchards and dotted with little chuches and villages. Another attraction is the Cave of Dhaskálio on the headland (but only accessible from the sea), which was inhabited in neolithic times and now is a show cave with dramatic stalactites.

Above: the valley of Vathí,
on Kálymnos, leads down
to a fjord-like inlet

KÁRPATHOS (▶ 16, TOP TEN)

KÁSOS

For those who want the taste of a Greek island barely touched by tourism, Kásos has to be the destination – provided, that is, that you can get there. The seas here are notoriously rough, as the several lighthouses indicate, and the ferry connections from Kárpathos and elsewhere can't always dock in the tiny main port of Frý. The alternative is to fly from Kárpathos in a light aircraft.

Kásos is the most southerly of the Dodecanese and has a surprisingly high population of 1,500, spread around its five main settlements. Fishing and farming are still the main activities, but there are a few simple hotels for the more adventurous travellers, and some reasonable beaches on the offshore islets of Armathiá and Makrá, to which local fishermen will be happy to take you.

74B1

Tourist Information (Maritre Tourist Agency) ☎ 0245 41232; Port Authority ☎ 0245 41288; Police ☎ 0245 41222

Occasional ferries to Kárpathos, Rhodes and some other Dodecanesian and Cycladic islands

KASTELLÓRIZO (MEGÍSTI)

This little island is tucked in less than 2km off the coast of Turkey, yet is more than 100km from its nearest Greek neighbour, Rhodes. It is barely 8km long, hence its affectionate alternative name of Megísti: 'the biggest'. It seems incredible to think that the population here was once as high as 14,000, as there is only one main town: Kastellórizo Town. Some attractive mansions line the quay, and the fish restaurants here are highly rated, but as you climb up the slopes away from the water you see more and more ruined mansions which tell of a much more prosperous past.

75F1

Port Authority ☎ 0241 49270; Police ☎ 0241 49333; Airport ☎ 0241 49241

Occasional ferries to Rhodes and Piréas, and some Cycladic and other Dodecanesian islands

There are no beaches and the swimming is not very tempting as the rocks are thick with sea urchins. There are walks across the rather rugged landscape to some deserted chapels and monasteries, but other than that it is a place to switch off, relax and do nothing.

The shimmering waters of the remote island of Kastellórizo

In the Know

If you only have a short time to visit the Greek Islands and would like to get a real flavour of them, here are some ideas:

Lunch in the shade of a tree in Pýrgos, on Tínos

Ways to Be a Local

Take a siesta – islanders wake early and stay up late, but compensate (especially in the hot summer months) by taking a siesta from about 2 to 5PM.

Ride on a bus. Island buses mix locals and visitors and give the latter a glimpse of local life.

Slow down: you may have to in the heat of high summer, but islanders take the relaxed approach to everything all year round.

Dress appropriately: cover up when visiting churches and monasteries.

Sing or dance when you're in the mood. The Greeks have no inhibitions about expressing their joy of life.

80

Don't compliment Turkey, or call Greek coffee Turkish coffee, or Greek Delight Turkish Delight, or gaze wistfully across to the mainland of Turkey and say how beautiful it is.

Take a ferry ride, if only from one island to another and back again. Ferries are the lifelines of the islands.

Be patient with children: Greeks are very tolerant of children, even when they are behaving badly.

Take a stroll. Join the Greeks in their evening *volta*, walking up and down just to see and be seen.

Eat late, as the Greeks do.

Good Places to Have Lunch

Anonymous (£)
✉ Antóni Trítsi 146, Argostóli, Kefalloniá
☎ 0671 22403. By the harbour, fresh fish and daily specials.

Eirína (£)
✉ Livádia, Tílos ☎ 0241 44206. Overlooks the water, away from the street, affable host and good home cooking.

Gkoúveris (£)
✉ Leofóros Voudoúri 20, Chalkída, Évvoia ☎ 0221 25769. On the waterfront, with fresh fish grilled outside.

O Gláros (£)
✉ Alykí Bay, Thásos ☎ 0593 53047. Sea

views and good fresh fish in a long-established restaurant.

Kondylénia's (£)
✉ Kamíni road, Ýdra Town, Ýdra ☎ 0298 53520. Panoramic views to the mainland, and some of the best food on the island.

Oneíro (£)
✉ Parapórti area, Náxos Town ☎ 0285 23846. Choose the roof garden for the views.

Oi Psarádes (£)
✉ Waterfront, Kondakaíika, Sámos ☎ 0273 32489. Great fish dishes served on terrace overlooking the sea.

Tólis (£)
✉ Pédi Bay, Sými ☎ 0241 71601. By the beach, lovely bay, good food.

Trapasélli's (£)
✉ Adamántas, Mílos ☎ 0287 22010. Best fish place on Mílos, right on the waterfront.

Troúllos (£)
✉ Troúllos Beach, Skiáthos ☎ 0427 49255. You can't get better than fresh fish served right by the beach.

Top Activities

Cycling: Information from the Greek Cycling Federation, Bouboulinas 28, Athens ☎ 01 883 1414.

Golf: Not an obvious choice for the Greek Islands but

there are courses on Corfu in the Ropá Valley (Corfu Golf Club ☎ 0663 94220) and on Rhodes (Afandou Golf Club ☎ 0241 51255).

Horse-riding: For details throughout Greece and the islands, contact the Hellenic Riding Club, Paradisou 18, Athens ☎ 01 682 6128.

Mountaineering: Many islands have high peaks that are certainly strenuous walks, but the only one to warrant a mountain shelter is Évvoia. Details from Greek Mountaineering Club, Milioni 5, 10673 Athens ☎ 01 364 5904.

Sailing: Information from the Hellenic Yachting Federation, Akti Navarchou Kountouridti 7, Piréas, Athens ☎ 01 413 7351.

Scuba diving: Permitted only in certain areas during daylight hours, so check locally. The permitted areas are on or near Kálymnos,

Renting a scooter, as here on Alónnisos, is one way to get about

Corfu, Kós, Léfkas, Mýkonos, Paxoí, Rhodes and Zákynthos. For further details contact the Union of Greek Diving Centres ☎ 01 922 9532.

Tennis: Tennis facilities are usually available in large resort hotels, and may be available for non-residents to use. Further details from the Greek Tennis Association (EFOA), Omirou 8, Athens ☎ 01 323 0412.

Walking: The islands are blessed with good walking but not with well-marked paths. Always try to get a local map and seek local advice. Blobs of red paint are the simple Greek way of marking a walking trail.

Watersports: : Facilities for windsurfing, waterskiing, parascending and other beach pursuits are widely available in all main resorts.

Windsurfing: More experienced windsurfers who want the best facilities and space away from the beginners should look to the Ionian Islands (Corfu, Lefkáda and Zákynthos

especially), and to Kós, Lésvos, Náxos and Sámos.

10
Seafood Dishes

To help you negotiate the island menus:

Astakós Lobster
Bakaliáros Cod
Barboúnia Red mullet
Garídes Shrimps
Glósses Sole
Kalamarákia Squid
Lavráki Sea bass
Marídes Whitebait
Mídia Mussels
Xifías Swordfish

10
Islands to Get Away From It All

 74C5

Odós Vas. Georgiou 1,
Kós Town ☎ 0242
26585/28724 ③
Mon–Fri 7:30–9, Sat–Sun
8:30–3; Port Authority
☎ 0242 26594; Airport
☎ 0242 51255; Tourist
Police ☎ 0242 26666

Daily to Rhodes,
Kálymnos, Léros, Pátmos
and Piréas, less frequent
to other Dodecanesian
and Cycladic islands.

**Archaeological Museum &
Castle of the Knights**
☎ 0242 28326;
③ Tue–Sun 8.30–3
Moderate

The Asklepíon
✉ 5km southwest of Kós
Town
☎ 0242 28763
③ Tue–Sun 8:30–3

KÓS   ✪✪

Kós and Rhodes are the two prime islands in the
Dodecanese for the mass tourist market, and there are
places on either where you could be almost anywhere in
the Mediterranean. By day the beaches are full of bronzing
bodies, and at night the bars and discos blare out loud
music. Yet on both islands there are also plenty of quieter
places left, and isolated coves where you can have the
beach to yourself and hear nothing but the sound of the
waves.

Such a place is not Kardámaina, a brash resort which it
is hard to identify as a former fishing village. It has a great
beach, and beaches are one of the island's attractions. Kós
Town mixes tourism with culture, as it has beaches and
Roman remains, an enjoyable **Archaeological Museum**
and the 15th-century **Castle of the Knights**. It also has an
ancient plane tree said to be one under which Hippocrates
once taught – although it is nowhere near old enough.

If you want to see the Greek face of Kós and escape
the packed resorts, head for the villages on the slopes of
Mount Díkeos, also called the Asfendioú. The island's
most important historical site is **Asklepíeío** (The Asklepion),
a shrine to Asklepios, the God of Healing. It dates back to
the 4th century BC and is worth seeing not just for the
remains of its white marble temples but also for the
impressive views over the island.

Old Kós Town

With your back to the plane tree under which Hippocrates is said to have taught, walk towards the harbour to your left but turn right to walk around the walls of the fortress.

A Knights' Castle was here in the early 14th century but the present building dates from the late 15th century.

Walk all the way round the castle walls returning to the plane tree, next to which is the 18th-century Loggia Mosque. Walk past the mosque and turn slightly left to walk by the ruins of the Ancient Agorá.

The Agorá is still being excavated, but some remains go back to the 3rd century BC. The remains were only uncovered after an earthquake in 1933. At the end of the Agorá is Plateía Eleftherías, where you can visit the Archaeological Museum, the Defterdor Mosque and, to the left, the market.

Walk down Filíta, to the left of the Cinema Orfeus, and turn right along 31 Martioú. On your right is the Roman Agorá. Beyond here turn left down Tsaldári which, after a bend in the road, takes you past the Ancient Gymnasium and Ancient Hippodrome, both on your left. Turn left at the end and you reach the entrance to the Ancient Stadium. Continue down Grigoríou and on your right you come to the Casa Romana, a private Roman villa from about the 3rd century AD. Turn left down Ioannídi, almost opposite the Casa Romana, and this crosses at an angle Kleopátras, where the Olympiáda makes a great lunch stop, before heading back down to the harbour to conclude the walk.

Distance
3km

Time
2–3 hours with stops

Start point
Hippocrates Tree

End point
Harbourfront

Lunch
Olympiáda (£)
✉ Kleopátras 2
☎ 0242 23031

Opposite: *the Temple of Apollo at The Asklepion*
Left: *the 18th-century minaret of the Defterdar Mosque in Kós Town*

83

🚩 74B6

ℹ️ In the Town Hall
☎ 0247 41250; Port
Authority ☎ 0247
41240

⛴ Occasional ferries to
Piréas and to some
Dodecanesian and
Cycladic islands

LEIPSOÍ ✪✪

Tiny Leipsoí (you could walk across it in an afternoon) claims to be the island of the nymph Calypso, who kept Homer's Odysseus here for seven years, so beguiled was he by her charms. Well, perhaps, but visitors are being beguiled in increasing numbers by Leipsoí's own charms. At the height of summer the island looks as though it might sink beneath the weight of visitors, swollen during the day by the visits of trippers from Pátmos and Léros. Outside July and August, however, Leipsoí returns to the sleepy ways of its 650 inhabitants, who go about their farming and fishing and let the handfuls of visitors go about their own ways too.

The island's only village, also called Leipsoí, is a dazzling little place of bright whites and blues, as the islanders, as well as being friendly, are known for being proud of their island and keep it looking pristine. There are waterfront tavernas, plenty of rooms to rent thanks to the summer invasion, a little museum of island artefacts, and several blue-domed churches, including Ágios Ioánnis. This contains what is said to be a miraculous icon, which Greek visitors to the island naturally go to see to seek the answers to their prayers. For those seeking less spiritual delights, there are some sandy beaches and little bays, but for real escape you can take a boat to the even smaller and quieter islands of Arkí and Maráthi.

Above: the blue dome of the church of Ágios Ioánnis is unmistakable above the main town of Leipsoí

LÉROS ✪✪

It has taken Léros a long time to enter the world of tourism, and in comparison with most islands it is still a slow starter. Its problem was one of image, as most Greeks associated its name with the leper colonies, prison camps and mental hospitals which have been located there in the not too distant past. Most would never dream of going there for a holiday. The lack of tourist infrastructure meant that there was little encouragement to overseas visitors either. That is starting to change, as foreign visitors discover its unpretentious charms, unknowing or unaffected by the unpleasant associations of its name. Its coastline is heavily indented, which provides plenty of sheltered coves for bathing and sun-worshipping; its interior is fairly green for most of the year; it has some great waterfront fish tavernas and its long musical tradition is still apparent in occasional late-night music sessions, when the dulcimer, pipes and other instruments may be produced to induce some dancing.

The main town is Plátanos, which has a lot going for it. Amongst its many attractions are: lovely views; some fine, neo-classical mansion houses beneath a Byzantine castle; a lively square, which acts as a focal point for local life, and some interesting old churches to explore. The church of the Megalochóri Kyrás Kástrou has a miraculous icon of the Virgin Mary, of which there seems to be no shortage in the Dodecanese. The main port is Lakkí, where there is a British military cemetery, and whose crumbling art deco houses may have an unsettling effect on the unsuspecting visitor. These are the remnants of Italian occupation, which locals have neither the inclination nor the money to renovate.

✚ 74B5
✉ Quayside, Lakkí
☎ 0247 22937; Port Authority ☎ 0247 22234
🚢 Daily to Piréas, Pátmos, Sámos, Kálymnos, Kós and Rhodes, less frequent to some Cycladic islands

A red-roofed windmill, surrounded by the waters of Ágia Marina on Léros island

+ 74C4

ℹ Enetikon Travel, Mandráki
☎ 0242 31180; Port
Authority ☎ 0242
31222

🚢 Daily in season to Rhodes
and Kós, less frequent to
some other
Dodecanesian and
Cycladic islands

NÍSYROS ✪✪✪

A day trip to Nísyros, taking in the crater of its volcano, has visitors wondering if they have landed on another planet. The crater cradles the midsummer heat and turns it into a cauldron, even by Greek standards, and the ground crunches beneath your feet, with clusters of sulphur crystals.

Most people only see Nísyros this way, on a boat trip from neighbouring Kós (► 82), but the island has much more to offer those who stay here. Accommodation can be found in or near the little port of Mandráki, which is postcard-pretty with its white houses with wooden balconies and its winding narrow streets. The north coast is where the small amount of tourist development has taken place and a coast road leads to little Loutrá and White Beach, and beyond that to the island's best beach at Paloí. To visit the crater, which still rumbles beneath your feet, head for the village of Nikiá and start your descent from there.

PÁTMOS (► 20, TOP TEN)

PSÉRIMOS ✪

The speck in the Aegean that is Psérimos is about half-way between Kós and Kálymnos. Day trips from both islands are popular, and in summer the numbers are high enough to swamp the allegedly peaceful little island that people have come to see: only about 70 people live here. There is one small cluster of houses, with a beach and small jetty, and those staying here tend to head off to one of the distant coves during the day, and return for a quiet evening, eating at one of the handful of tavernas.

+ 74C5

🚢 Daily excursions in
season to/from Kós and
Kálymnos

The volcanic crater of Nísyros is unique in the Greek Islands, but hasn't erupted since 1522

Exploring Rhodes Old Town

Starting at Mandráki Harbour, this short walk guides you to some of the best features of the Old Town of Rhodes.

Begin at the harbour entrance.

The Colossus of Rhodes may have stood astride the harbour entrance, but there is no historical evidence for this.

Walk along the harbour front with the town on your right. Ahead is the start of the Old Town. Beyond the market on the right, cross at the traffic lights. Continue on through the Eleftherias Gate.

The road swings left and leaves the Old Town. On your left is the Temple of Aphrodite.

Walk ahead. On your right is the Museum of Decorative Arts. Pass this and turn right.

This is Ippodon, the Street of the Knights.

Go to the top, pass the Palace of the Grand Masters on the right, and turn left.

On your left is the Sulimaniye Mosque (mosque of Suleiman), opposite the Ottoman Library.

Turn right down Ippodamou, to the end, where the road swings left. Turn right at the T-junction, through the gate.

Leaving the Old Town here lets you appreciate the immense city walls.

Turn left outside the gate, and follow the road. Turn next left into the Gate of St John. Go left at the first T-junction and follow Pithagora, to Plateía Sokrátous. Turn left up Sokrátous, then at a crossroads by a café, turn left down Meneklèous.

Distance
2km

Time
2hr with stops

Start pointt
Mandráki Harbour

End point
Odûs Meneklèous

Lunch
Romeo (£)
✉ Meneklèous 7-9
☎ 0241 25186

Above: *Mandraki harbour*
Below: *Sulimaniye Mosque*

A scooter bumps down the Street of the Knights

🔲 75E4

🚢 Daily to Piréas, Kálymnos, Kós, Léros, Sámos and Pátmos, less frequent to most other Dodecanesian and Cycladic islands

ℹ️ Plateía Rimínis ☎ 0241 35945

Palace of the Grand Masters
✉️ Ippodon
☎️ 0241 23559
🕐 Tue–Fri 8–7, Sat–Sun 8–3, Mon 12:30–7
♿ Limited
💶 Expensive

Mosque of Suleiman
✉️ Orféos Sokrátous
🕐 Under renovation at present

Ródos (Rhodes)

The biggest island in the Dodecanese is the country's most popular holiday destination, a fact that you cannot miss if you drive from the airport into Rhodes Town. On your right is an endless row of hotels, shops and bars, and on your left endless rows of beach umbrellas and bronzing bodies. Continue on around the coast (Rhodes Town is on the northernmost tip of the island) and the scene remains the same. To be fair, this is where the bulk of the rampant tourist development has taken place. There are many quieter parts of the island, and the capital town itself is one of the most fascinating of all the island ports.

What to See on Rhodes

RHODES TOWN

While Rhodes New Town is as brash and busy as any other modern Greek city, with the thundering of traffic and the honking of ships' horns in the port, Rhodes Old Town provides some quieter corners … when you can find them. The Old Town is contained within its imposing walls, which were built in 1330 and are on average almost 12m thick, running for 4km around the old part of the town. They are being extensively renovated and at present access is by guided tour only (Tue and Sat at 2:30PM from the front of the **Palace of the Grand Masters**).

The Castle of the Knights of St John watches over Líndos, first inhabited around 2000BC

The grand Palace was also built in the 14th century for the Knights of St John, and now contains exhibitions about the history of the island and of Rhodes Town in particular. Outside is the magnificent medieval Street of the Knights, one of the finest medieval streets in Europe. Other attractions are the 1523 **Mosque of Suleiman**, the town's **Archaeological Museum**, the several grand gates giving access to the Old Town and a warren of back streets where most visitors seldom venture but which repay the risk of getting lost in them.

Archaeological Museum

- ✉ Plateía Mouseíou
- ☎ 0241 27657
- 🕐 Tue–Fri 8–7, Sat–Sun 8–3, Mon 12:30–7
- ♿ None
- 🍴 Moderate

LÍNDOS ● ● ●

Half-way down the east coast of Rhodes, beyond the island's busiest resort at Faliráki, is the dazzling village of Líndos. Its whitewashed houses sparkle beneath the **Acropolis** which stands 125m high and is topped by a temple which dates back to the 4th century BC. Líndos's back streets are a maze of white houses, elegant doorways, pebbled courtyards and trailing bougainvillaea. Add to this a lovely long beach, and you have the perfect setting for a popular resort. Líndos is incredibly busy, but is one of those places which retains its appeal despite the crowds.

- ✚ 75E3
- ℹ Tourist Information
  - ☎ 0244 31900

Acropolis

- ☎ 0244 31258;
- 🕐 Tue–Fri 8–2:40, Sat–Sun 8:30–2:40, Mon 2:30–6:40
- ♿ None
- 🍴 Expensive

THE VALLEY OF THE BUTTERFLIES ● ●

Conveniently for summer visitors, the valley of Petaloúdes has its own summer visitors: millions (literally) of Jersey tiger-moths which swarm here from June until September. They are attracted by the resin from the particular trees which grow in the valley, and provide a popular day trip from the coastal resorts. The valley itself is worth seeing, being green and leafy, and has pleasant walks well away from where the tourist buses deposit their visitors.

- ✚ 75E3
- 🕐 Apr–Sep daily 9–5
- ♿ None
- 🍴 Cheap

SÝMI (➤ 22, TOP TEN)

TÍLOS (➤ 25, TOP TEN)

Overleaf: *one of Greece's greatest pleasures – a supper at sunset, with a view to the sea, here at Chóra on Alónnisos*

DID YOU KNOW?

The Colossus of Rhodes was one of the Seven Wonders of the Ancient World. It was a 40m-high statue of Helios, the Sun God – the ancient Greeks called the island 'more beautiful than the sun' – but it almost certainly did not straddle the harbour entrance as raditionally depicted. It probably stood at the Temple of Apollo, now the site of the Palace of the Grand Masters.

Where To...

retsina wine

Above: the locals love a game of backgammon
Right: their taste for retsina is not always shared by the tourists

Ionian Islands

Prices

Approximate prices for a three-course meal for one person, without drinks or service:

£ = under 5,000dr
££ = 5,000-10,000dr
£££ = over 10,000dr

Itháki

Gregory's (£)

Some way out of the island's capital but you can get a boat to take you there to sample the daily catch, fresh fish and hearty local wine, straight from the barrel.

⊠ Paleó Karábo, Váthi ☎ 0674 32573 Ⓖ Daily breakfast, lunch and dinner till late

Trehadíri Taverna(£)

Wonderful family-run place, where the wife cooks and the husband serves. Basic menu with such dishes as *moussaka* and grilled meats, but all done with great care and delicious results.

⊠ Váthi ☎ 0674 33066 Ⓖ Daily 6PM–midnight

Kefalloniá

Anonymous (£)

This little family-run place is right on the harbour and limits its menu to a few daily specials, plus the conventional grills and fresh fish.

⊠ Antóni Trítsi 146, Argostóli ☎ 0671 22403 Ⓖ Daily noon–midnight

Faros (£)

Right on the waterfront in this picturesque port, Faros ('The Lighthouse') includes the island speciality of *kreatópita* (Kefallonian meat pie) on their varied menu.

⊠ Paralía, Fiskárdo ☎ 0674 41277 Ⓖ Daily 11AM–11PM

Oi Kalyva (£)

This homely place in the town centre has a typical plain Greek menu, with salads and grilled meats, but it does it well, and the owners add their own warmth.

⊠ Plateía Valiánou, Argostóli ☎ 0671 24849 Ⓖ Daily lunch and dinner

Old Plaka (£)

Typical open-all-hours Greek place, but a smarter clientele in the evenings for the reasonably priced but tasty Greek fare. Pork stuffed with garlic is a succulent house speciality.

⊠ Metaxa 1, Argostóli ☎ 0671 24849 Ⓖ Daily 9AM–2AM

Kérkyra (Corfu)

Aegli (££)

Great place on Corfu Town's fashionable Listón, where people come to see and be seen. The location adds to the price but the food is exceptionally good, and includes many island specialities. Try their *sofrito* (veal in a garlic sauce).

⊠ Kapodístriou 23 ☎ 0661 31949 Ⓖ Daily 10:30AM–midnight

Chambor (£££)

The best and most expensive restaurant in Corfu Town, lovely location near Plateía Dimarcheíou, and food that ranges from superbly done *moussaka* to island specialities such as *bourdetto* (fish in a tomato and garlic sauce).

⊠ Guildford 71, Corfu Town ☎ 0661 39031 Ⓖ Daily 9AM–2AM

Grill Room Chrissomális (£)

Very basic, much frequented by locals rather than tourists, and you will get the best of grilled meals at reasonable prices. Friendly service, too.

⊠ Theotóki 6, Corfu Town ☎ 0661 30342 Ⓖ Daily noon–midnight

Iannis Taverna (£)

Great local place well away from the touristy resorts with a changing menu according to what's fresh: try their excellent *stifado*.

✉ **Iássonos, Anemómilos, Corfu Town** ☎ 0116 33061 🕐 Mon–Sat 8:30PM–midnight

Sossi Fish Taverna (££)

Whatever fish is in season, it'll be here. You will have to elbow your way through local people, who know that this is the place for fish: bream, snapper, red mullet, whitebait, sardines, swordfish, squid and octopus.

✉ **Mandoúki, Corfu Town** 🕐 Daily 8:30PM–midnight

Venetian Well (££)

In a beautiful quiet square, this serves some of the most inventive food on the island, mixing Greek with Middle and Far Eastern dishes to great effect.

✉ **Platía Kremásti, Corfu Town** ☎ 0661 44761 🕐 Mon–Sat noon–midnight

Yioryás Taverna (£)

Authentically basic Greek taverna where locals call in for a chat and the more adventurous tourists savour the atmosphere. Unpretentious food, mainly grills, but of the best quality and a terrific lively atmosphere.

✉ **Guildford 16, Corfu Town** ☎ 0661 37147 🕐 Daily 11:30AM–midnight

Lefkáda

Miramare (£)

Pleasant place to eat with good sea views, and hearty meals served with typical Greek generosity. Vegetables are grown in their own garden.

✉ **Paralía, Vassilikí, Lefkáda Town** ☎ 0645 31138 🕐 Daily 8:30AM–2AM

Regantos (£)

A place that's popular in Lefkáda Town must be good, as there aren't many tourists and the locals know what's what. Try the meat stews, sausages and kebabs, which Lefkáda is noted for.

✉ **Dimárhou Verióti 17, Lefkáda Town** 🕐 Daily 7PM–11

Paxoí

Taka-Taka (£)

Long-established favourite which specialises in grilled meat and fresh fish. Friendly owners and a lovely garden eating area, covered in vines.

✉ **Gaïos** ☎ 0662 31323 🕐 Daily 11:30AM–10PM

Vassíli's (£)

Right on the lovely little harbour at Longós, this restaurant looks very ordinary but serves up the best food on the island. Best to book at busy times.

✉ **Waterfront, Longós** ☎ 0662 31587 🕐 Some lunchtimes, dinner daily from 7PM

Zákynthos

Mantalena (£)

Arguably the best restaurant on the island, family-run and serving traditional recipes handed down over the generations. Complimentary *ouzo* welcomes evening diners, and they make their own wine too.

✉ **Alikanás** ☎ 0695 83487 🕐 Daily 9AM–midnight

Oréa Héllas (£)

Long-established favourite with the locals, serving island specialities such as roast pork or *sáltsa* (substantial beef stew).

✉ **Ioánnou Logothétou 11, Zákynthos Town** ☎ 0695 28622 🕐 Daily 7AM–1AM

Opening Hours

Greek opening hours are flexible. In some countries if a restaurant says that it will open at 7pm then it will open within a couple of minutes of that time. In Greece – well, it might open at 6:30, it might open at 7:30, it depends on how busy it is, what's on the menu, how the owner feels, whether he has to visit his cousin that day, or whatever. Visitors must be equally flexible.

93

Saronic & Northern Aegean Islands

The Kitchen

In a taverna you will be expected to wander into the kitchen to see what's cooking, and whichever of the staff is more fluent in languages will show and explain what is in the various pots. If choosing fish you are advised to go into the kitchen to pick the specific piece that you want. In more up-market restaurants, the thought of you visiting the kitchen will be frowned on, just as you would never do so in France or Italy, say.

Alónnisos

Astrofengiá (£)

Wonderful views at this popular restaurant which is about as high as you can go in the Old Town. The evenings get lively if the feeling is right, and the food ranges from simple (grilled fish steaks and stuffed tomatoes) to more sophisticated (artichoke hearts with a cream and dill sauce).

✉ Old Alónnisos ☎ 0424 65182
🕐 Daily 6PM–midnight

Chíos

Apolaisi (££)

Residents of Chíos Town happily travel the 10km or so to this fishing village and its excellent fish taverna, which overlooks the water. Romantic setting and you'll get the best of what's been caught in the village that day.

✉ Ayía Ermióni ☎ 0271 31359
🕐 Daily 5PM–midnight

Theodosiou Ouzéri (£)

If you fancy more casual dining by the waterfront, then this *ouzéri* offers a good selection of *meze* dishes which would make up a meal, with pastries and ice-creams on offer, too.

✉ Paralía, Chíos Town 🕐 Daily 5PM–midnight

Lésvos

Arion (£)

Right on the sea, so a great setting for traditional Greek fare such as *moussaka*, stuffed peppers, fish steaks. Nothing fancy but it is all well prepared.

✉ Waterfront, Eressós ☎ 0251 53384 🕐 Daily lunch and dinner

Averof 1841 Grill (£)

Simple little grill place on the port, and a safe bet if you are spending time in the island's capital. There are some mediocre places around, but not this one. Good *souvlaki* and chops, and a few other standard Greek dishes.

✉ Koundouriótou, Mytilíni 🕐 Daily 11:30AM–11:30PM

The Captain's Table (£)

Right on the harbour, and the house special is a huge 'Captain's Plate' of mixed seafood, but there are also simple grills, vegetarian options, Italian and more exotic dishes, too.

✉ Harbour, Mólyvos ☎ 0253 71241 🕐 Daily 11AM–1AM. Closed winter

Póros

Caravella (££)

Down by the port this place has both good fish dishes, including slightly unusual items such as octopus salad, and heartier meat dishes like *stifado*. Slightly expensive because of the setting, but good quality.

✉ Paralía, Póros Town ☎ 0298 23666 🕐 Daily 10AM–1AM

Sámos

Stelios (£)

This well-established taverna specialises in traditional Samian recipes, as well as other Greek favourites, such as the ever-popular *stifado*.

✉ Kephalopoúlou, Sámos Town ☎ 0273 23639 🕐 Daily 11AM–midnight

Taverna Ávgo Tou Kókora (£)

Lovely waterfront location for this slightly more upmarket eating place, which offers a bewildering variety of *meze* dishes that can be well recommended, though the more substantial single dishes such as fresh fish or steaks are on offer too.

✉ **Kokkári** ☎ 0273 92113 ⊙ **Daily noon–1AM**

Varka (££)

This *ouzéri* has been funded by the local community, and the food is as good as the setting is unusual: Varka means 'boat' and this is indeed a former fishing boat that has been converted. Expect the best of the local fish, although *souvlaki*, chops and steaks are also available, but go for the *meze*: they do a surprisingly good range of tasty nibbles.

✉ **Paralía, Pythagório** ☎ 0273 61636 ⊙ **May–Oct daily noon–midnight**

Skíathos
Kampoureli Ouzéri (££)

In the great bustling Greek *ouzéri* tradition, serving *meze*, a range of nibbles to eat with your *ouzo*, such as octopus, squid and olives. You can also have a more substantial meal if you wish.

✉ **Paralía, Skíathos Town** ☎ 0427 21112 ⊙ **Daily noon–1AM**

The Windmill (££)

Right at the top of the eastern hill in the main town is this smart restaurant whose food is as special as its setting. Chicken with bourbon and chilli is just one example of the unusual combinations that you won't find in your average Greek taverna. There is a range of tempting desserts which includes poached pears and a comprehensive wine list.

✉ **Skíathos Town** ☎ 0427 21105 ⊙ **Daily 7PM–11PM**

Skópelos
Taverna T'Agnanti (£)

This family-run little taverna is one of those unpretentious places that are a delight to find in the islands: great atmosphere, friendly hosts, inexpensive and good examples of standard Greek dishes: squid, grills, chops, *moussaka*.

✉ **Glóssa** ☎ 0424 33606 ⊙ **Daily 7AM–midnight**

Skýros
Kristina's Restaurant (££)

Austrian Kristina is trying to combine a more modern touch, such as a generous number of vegetarian dishes and a variety of breads, with Greek traditions. Her speciality has become chicken fricassée.

✉ **Skýros Town** ☎ 0222 91778 ⊙ **Mon–Sat 7PM–midnight**

Spétses
Exedra (££)

Right on the Old Harbour, its prices are a little high but the standard of the food makes it worth paying. They do many of the island's seafood specialities such as *argó* (a shrimp/lobster/feta cheese casserole).

✉ **Paleó Limáni, Spétses Town** ☎ 0298 73497 ⊙ **Daily lunch and dinner**

Ýdra
The Garden (££)

Superb garden setting and food to match, as proved by the fact that you will have to book at busy times. Swordfish *souvlaki* is one of the house specialities, but there are a number of meat and vegetarian options too.

✉ **Ýdra Town** ☎ 0298 52329 ⊙ **Daily 7PM–midnight**

Tavernas

Tavernas tend to be less smart than places which call themselves restaurants. In a restaurant you will probably get a proper wine glass, a napkin and a linen tablecloth. In a taverna you are likely to get a little tumbler for the wine and a disposable paper cloth, on which the waiter may well work out your bill. But there are no rules. Expect anything in the Greek islands.

Cyclades

Tipping
Greek menus normally have two lines of prices, one slightly lower than the other. The lower price is 'without tax', which is purely theoretical as they have to charge tax on their prices and you will be billed the higher price. Service is not normally included, so it is usual to round the bill up by about 10 per cent or so, though no-one counts exactly and 'keep the change' is normal.

Mýkonos
Chez Cat'rine (£££)
One of only a handful of places in the Cyclades which is in the upper price bracket and where you would be well advised to book. Greek dishes are given a love and attention normally seen only in France, and there are some French appetisers on the menu. Main courses tend towards seafood, but always prepared and presented with flair.
✉ **Ágios Yerásimos, Chóra, Mýkonos Town** ☎ **0289 22169** 🕐 **Daily 6:30PM–midnight**

Niko's (£)
If the island's relentless and expensive sophistication is not to your taste, try this unpretentious but always busy little taverna which serves fish, *souvlaki*, grills and other conventional dishes. Low on cost, high on atmosphere.
✉ **Chóra, Mýkonos Town** 🕐 **Daily noon–11PM**

Sesame Kitchen (£)
An addition to the welcome Greek trend to open more health-conscious and vegetarian restaurants. The Sesame isn't totally vegetarian, as their popular chicken pies demonstrate, but it does offer vegetarian *moussaka*, brown rice and many vegetarian options. Try their delicious spinach pie.
✉ **Plateía Tría Pigadía, Chóra, Mýkonos Town** ☎ **0289 24710** 🕐 **Daily 7PM–12:30AM**

Náxos
Faros (££)
Another example of a restaurant where foreign influence (in this case German) has combined with Greek tradition and ingredients to provide an astonishingly wide menu. An old Greek stand-by, meatballs, which can be very uninspiring, are given a new lease of life with a goulash-style sauce, while there are some original dishes too, such as liver Berlin-style.
✉ **Paralía, Chóra, Náxos Town** ☎ **0285 23325** 🕐 **Daily 8AM–4AM**

Nikos (£)
Nikos is owned by fisherman Nikos Katsayannis, and therefore fish on the menu is guaranteed fresh. Nikos, more often than not, also has some unusual varieties on offer, not always with a suitable English name. There are plenty of meat and vegetarian options, too, on a wide menu, and just as wide is the wine list, which concentrates on wines from Náxos and the other Cycladic islands.
✉ **Paralía, Chóra, Náxos Town** ☎ **0285 23153** 🕐 **Daily 8AM–2AM**

Páros
Aligariá (£)
Lovely little place run by a gifted cook, Elizabeth Nikolousou, who knows how to serve up old favourites such as *moussaka* or stuffed tomatoes, with an attention to detail that reminds you how good they can be when done properly.
✉ **Plateía Aligari, Parikiá** ☎ **0284 22026** 🕐 **Daily lunch and dinner**

To Kyma (£)
'The Wave' is new, and run by two French women who serve up an international menu, including Thai, Chinese, French and even

Scottish dishes alongside Greek favourites such as *moussaka*, squid, stuffed vegetables and lobster.

✉ **Ágioi Anárgyroi Beach** ☎ **0284 51735** ⏰ **Daily lunch and dinner**

Lalula (££)

Greek island cooking is being influenced by the many overseas visitors who take up residence here and try to blend the best of Greek cooking with the latest international trends. This stylish German-run place does just that, adding more vegetarian options and a lighter touch to traditional meat and fish dishes.

✉ **Náousa** ☎ **0284 51547** ⏰ **Daily 7PM–midnight**

Levantis (£)

The name of this friendly little taverna, with its tables under the trailing vines, indicates a nod towards the flavours of the Middle East, and of Cyprus, with the use of yoghurts, apricots and nuts, and tender chicken dishes. There are always several daily specials, and the best kind of hospitable Greek service.

✉ **Parikiá** ☎ **0284 23613** ⏰ **Wed–Mon 7PM–2AM**

Sífnos

Apostoli's (£)

This taverna on the pedestrianised main street is as simple and as Greek – and as leisurely – as they come. They do have an unusually large range of vegetarian dishes, as well as straightforward but tasty *souvlaki*, *moussaka* and other favourites.

✉ **Apollonía** ☎ **0284 31186** ⏰ **Daily noon–midnight**

Captain Andreas (£/££)

If your needs are simple – the best local fish, grilled – then the Captain Andreas, right on the beach, is the place to come. The eponymous owner catches most of the menu himself, and buys the best from his fellow fishermen, and the taste and setting don't come any better.

✉ **By the beach, Kamáres** ☎ **0284 32356** ⏰ **Daily 1–5, 7:30–3**

Tó Liotrívi (££)

Sífnos is said to produce the finest chefs in Greece, and the chef here, Yiannis Yiorgoulis, is said to be the finest one who has actually stayed on the island. His ordinary dishes are extraordinary, and his special dishes are very special indeed. For an introduction to his distinctive culinary style, try a simple but unusual and delicious *kaparosaláta* (caper salad), and you'll know why this place is so popular, even though its prices remain very reasonable.

✉ **Artemóna** ☎ **0284 32051** ⏰ **Daily noon–midnight**

Sofia's (£)

The opening hours tell you this is a Greek establishment and makes few concessions to the foreign tourists. There is an attractive outdoor seating area overlooking the beach, making for a great atmosphere in which to enjoy the simple but good dishes such as meat grills, stuffed peppers and grilled fish.

✉ **On the beach, Platís Yialós** ☎ **0284 31890** ⏰ **Daily 9pm–1am**

Informality

Like most Mediterranean countries, Greece is very informal when it comes to eating out. Few people dress formally because of the climate, and a casual T-shirt or short-sleeved shirt will be perfectly OK in most places. Even in smart restaurants, there are seldom any dress rules, so just dress comfortably and don't worry about wearing a collar and tie.

Ordering

The Greek tradition is not like the American or Western European tradition, where you order a starter and a main course, and they come one after the other. Greek dishes tend to come when they are ready, so if you have a hot starter but a pre-prepared main course, the main course may come first. Or everything may come together – starters, main course, side-salads, potatoes, vegetables. If you have any specific preference, you must make it clear to the waiter when ordering.

Sýros

Cavo d'Oro (£)

Ignore the Italian name, this is Greek seafood at its best. Right on the harbour, the fish virtually jump out of the boats and into the kitchen, where you can choose which one you want and whether to have it fried or grilled. Squid and octopus dishes also feature, with a few other Greek standards, though why come to a fish restaurant and not eat fish?

✉ **Paralía, Ermoúpolis** ☎ **0281 81440** 🕐 **Daily 11AM–midnight**

Thíra

1800 (££)

One of the best places in this dramatically set town where you can watch the sunset and eat good food, such as chicken in a walnut sauce and the best of the catch from the harbour down below... a long way down below!

✉ **Nikólaos Nomikós, Oía** ☎ **0286 71485** 🕐 **Daily 6PM–midnight**

Agiris (£)

In the village of Kamári rather than the beach resort, this taverna stays open all year, so relies on local custom – a good sign. Don't expect anything too imaginative, but what it does it does exceptionally well, and stuffed chicken has become a house speciality.

✉ **Kamári** ☎ **0286 31795** 🕐 **Daily 6PM–midnight**

Aris (££)

In a town where 'international' menus are all too common, this upmarket place, run by a chef (Aris Ziras) who worked at the Athens Hilton, offers the best of modern Greek cuisine. Old favourites such as *moussaka* are superbly done, and there is a large range of imaginative *meze* dishes, often good meals in themselves.

✉ **Agíou Miná** ☎ **0286 22840** 🕐 **Daily midday–1AM**

Katina (£)

If you can face the trek down to the harbour at Oía – or rather face the climb back up again after a fine evening meal (though you can always ring for a taxi) – then Katina's is a great place for seafood, and it's right down beside the sea.

✉ **Oía Port** ☎ **0286 71280** 🕐 **Daily 11AM–1AM**

Meridiana (£)

Great views out over the caldera of Thíra, as well as the island, this relaxed place has an international menu including Thai dishes, pastas and even paella, for those who want a change from Greek food. It also has a list of excellent Thíra specialities, for those who prefer the best regional cooking.

✉ **Ypapantís, Thíra Town** ☎ **0286 23427** 🕐 **Daily lunch and dinner**

Tínos

Leftéris (£)

There is a pleasant courtyard setting for this lively place where diners are usually dancing before the night is out. The wide-ranging menu includes fresh fish and traditional dishes such as *stifado, moussaka* and *dolmades*.

✉ **Harbour, Tínos Town** ☎ **0283 23013** 🕐 **Daily 11AM–midnight**

Dodecanese

Kálymnos

Barba Petros (£)

This distinctive place at the north end of the harbour is easy to spot, as a boat hangs outside the entrance. Fresh fish is grilled on olive-wood charcoal, or you can enjoy Greek island specialities such as squid stuffed with a delicious mix of spinach, cheese and herbs. Barba Petros is open all year and has to please the locals, which it invariably does.

✉ **Plateía Diamántis, Póthia** ☎ **0243 29678** ◉ **Daily 11AM–midnight**

Domus Roof Garden Restaurant (£)

The Domus has a spendid setting overlooking the beach and the Aegean, and fortunately food to match. Ordinary dishes such as *dolmades* and *moussaka* are exceptionally well done, and there are plenty of surprising inclusions, such as Armenian lamb, cooked with yoghurt. Very warm welcome.

✉ **Kantoúni** ☎ **0243 47959** ◉ **Daily lunch and dinner**

Taverna Ksefteris (£)

This taverna is an island institution, handed down through several generations of the same family. You won't get nouvelle cuisine but you will get tasty *dolmades*, hearty stews and a generous welcome.

✉ **Christós, Póthia** ☎ **0243 28642** ◉ **Daily 11:30AM–11PM**

Kós

Olympiada (£)

In a town that is full of below-average tourist tavernas, here is a treat. It's a genuine no-nonsense Greek place serving good food at cheap prices and without employing anyone to stand outside and try to persuade you to come in. Try a simple *souvlaki* or one of the many vegetable dishes.

✉ **Kleopátras 2, Kós Town** ☎ **0242 23031** ◉ **Daily 11AM–11PM**

Platános (£)

With the best setting in town, right next to the Hippocrates plane tree that gives this restaurant its name, the Platános could easily have decided to mass-cater for mass-market tourists who visit the town just once. Instead it offers unusual Greek dishes such as octopus *stifado*, with international variety such as Indonesian fillet steak, and most summer evenings there is live music which makes you want to linger.

✉ **Plateía Platános, Kós Town** ☎ **0242 28991** ◉ **Daily noon–11:30PM**

Taverna Mavromátis (£)

The Mavromáti brothers who run this taverna take no easy options but cater for Greek palates as well as those of overseas visitors. Deep-fried cheese is delicious, as are the tender grilled meat dishes, and of course there is always fresh fish. Lovely setting, right by the sea.

✉ **Psalídi beach** ☎ **0242 22433** ◉ **Daily 9AM–midnight. Closed winter**

Leipsoí

Delphini (£)

'Keep it simple' is the theme of this family-run taverna, which also manages to 'keep it tasty' too. The menu will have fish, bought daily from the fisherman, plenty of

Afterwards

Most Greek eating places have a limited dessert menu, usually restricted to a fruit salad or some ice-cream. The common habit in Greece is to move on from a restaurant to a bar or café for your coffee, perhaps a brandy, and some ice-cream or other dessert. Many cafés will have a display case full of the sticky-sweet cakes that the Greeks love so much.

Children

Greeks eat as families, and children are part of the family so they too will join any group eating out. If there are several children then a charming Greek custom is to give them their own separate table, next to the grown-ups. Most Greek children therefore quickly learn to order for themselves and, in family-run tavernas on the islands, children just as quickly learn how to wait on table and take your orders!

conventional dishes but a few slightly less common ones too, like deep-fried aubergines served with a garlic dip.

⊠ Leipsoí Town ☎ 0247 41257
🕐 Daily noon–midnight

Léros
Finikas (£)

Archetypal Greek taverna, with tables by the water's edge or behind in the shaded garden for lunch on hot days. Try their grilled dishes, stuffed peppers or *moussaka*.

⊠ Paralía, Alínda, Léros
☎ 0247 22695 🕐 Daily
9AM–11:30PM

Pátmos
Olympia (£)

Open all year round and appealing more to locals than visitors, the Olympia provides some unusual choices such as octopus baked in the oven, and for dessert their home-made walnut cake.

⊠ Plateía Theofakósta, Chóra
☎ 0247 31543 🕐 Mon–Sat
lunch and dinner

The Patmian House (££)

Book at busy times for the best restaurant on the island, and one of the best in Greece. A beautifully restored 17th-century building is the backdrop to fine food. Conventional starters such as *taramasalata* and spinach pie are home-made and mouthwateringly good, as are main dishes like, perhaps, a rabbit *stifado* with juniper berries. Dining experiences like this are rare in the Greek islands, so book in busy periods.

⊠ Chóra ☎ 0247 31180 🕐
Daily 7PM–midnight

To Pyrofáni (£)

This fish taverna buys its ingredients direct from the local fishermen, so you may get lobster, swordfish, tuna or mullet, depending on what's in season – but whatever it is, it will be fresh, and simply grilled.

⊠ Paralía, Skála, Pátmos
☎ 0247 31539 🕐 Daily lunch
and dinner

Ródos (Rhodes)
Alexis (£££)

Established over 40 years ago and still in the same family, this is one of the best fish restaurants in the Dodecanese. You will see seafood here you don't commonly see on menus (sea urchins for one example), and the best of the catch from the harbour. Given the amount of fish that comes through Rhodes harbour, that means the highest standard indeed. All vegetables are also organically grown by the owners. It is expensive but well worth it.

⊠ Sokrátous 18, Rhodes Town
☎ 0241 29347 🕐 Mon–Sat
lunch and dinner

Cleo's (£)

There are so many mediocre places in the Old Town, besieged these days as it is by hordes of tourists, but you can slip away from the main street, Sokrátous, and you find some pleasant surprises like this tasteful Italian restaurant, where you can still sample the local fish, cooked in an Italian-style, if you are not in the mood for pasta.

⊠ Agíou Fanouríou 17, Rhodes
Old Town ☎ 0241 28415 🕐
Daily 12–12

Kioupia (££)

The fixed-price menu of 8,000dr keeps this in the medium price range but make sure you go with an appetite. After a choice of soups you will be faced with a table full of tempting *meze* dishes, all of which you will want to eat, forgetting that the substantial and wonderfully cooked main course is yet to come. Remember, too, the mouth-watering dessert menu. One of the very best restaurants in the Greek islands.

✉ Trís village, Rhodes Town ☎ 0241 91824 ◉ Mon–Sat 8PM–midnight

Mavríkos (££)

An institution in the town's main square for over sixty years, Mavríkos cooks traditional Greek dishes, such as oven-baked lamb or assorted *meze* with a little French flair from time spent in France by their first chef. The traditions continue, and you would be advised to book ahead at busy periods.

✉ Líndos ☎ 0244 31232 ◉ Daily noon–midnight

Palia Istoria (££)

This award-winning restaurant is one of the best in the town, and not known to too many visitors as it is some way out of the centre. It's well worth the effort, though, and the extra cost. Their *meze* are renowned, including unusual options such as beetroot with walnuts, while main courses could be either a simple succulent roast pork to a pricier lobster spaghetti.

✉ Mitropóleos 108, Ammos, Rhodes Town ☎ 0241 32421 ◉ Daily 7PM–midnight

Yiannis (£)

In a town filled with poor-quality tavernas aimed at fleecing the thousands of gullible tourists, it's a pleasure to find a cheap and cheerful place where genuine Greek hospitality has not been lost. The same dishes feature as elsewhere (*moussaka*, stuffed tomatoes, *souvlaki*) but the standard is good, the portions generous and the prices reasonable.

✉ Appélou 41, Rhodes Town ☎ 0241 36535 ◉ Daily 9AM–midnight

Sými

Georgio's (£)

This island institution is as much drama as dining experience, with people queueing for tables, waiters running round with trays full of food, diners wandering into the kitchen, others waiting to pay and being offered titbits by the eccentric owner. Georgio may decide to play some music, if the mood takes him, and leave his staff to cope with the customers. This aside, the food is still good too.

✉ Chorió ◉ Daily, dinner only

Trata (£)

The Trata looks no different from many other tavernas around the harbour at Sými, but the standard of food is exceptional, and the owner keeps his eye on everything and runs a good place. The fresh fish is really excellent, and the home-made spinach pies superb. Pop into the kitchen to see what's cooking.

✉ Yialós ☎ 0241 71841 ◉ Daily 11AM–midnight

Brandy

In Greece the name of the leading make of brandy, Metaxa, has become synonymous with the drink itself, so people invariably ask for a Metaxa rather than a brandy. The quality of the drink is graded by the number of stars. One-star is rough, three-star is tolerable, and seven-star begins to compare in smoothness with brandies from France or Spain.

Ionian Islands

Room Rates
By law, all Greek hotels should display the room rate in the room itself. This is usually pinned to the back of the door and will be an official document, signed by the Tourist Police, and showing rates at different times of the year. You may have been able to strike a good deal with the owner, but, if you are being charged more than the official rate, you should ask why. There may be a legitimate explanation, but if you are suspicious contact the Tourist Police.

Itháki
Mentor (£)
A surprisingly smart little hotel right on the harbour of this island which is not swamped with visitors. The family owners keep it spotless, and there is a roof terrace with a bar for an evening drink overlooking the water.
✉ **Váthi** ☎ **0674 32433 fax 0674 32293**

Kefalloniá
Filoxenía (£/££)
Right on the seafront of this beautiful little port is a restored villa with traditional furniture, but inevitably a little pricey.
✉ **Fiskárdo** ☎ **0674 41319**

White Rocks (£££)
One of the best hotels on the island with its own beach, good facilities and not too far from Árgostoli. Smart-casual rather than super-plush, and closed in winter.
✉ **Platys Yíalos, Lássi, Árgostoli** ☎ **0671 28332 fax 0671 28755**

Kérkyra (Corfu)
Bella Venezia (££)
Reasonably priced restored Neo-classical mansion, a short walk from the town centre. Rooms have high ceilings and are comfortable without being luxurious. Very friendly and helpful staff.
✉ **Zampéli 4, Corfu Town** ☎ **0661 46500 fax 0661 20708**

Cavalieri (£££)
This is almost on the seafront and upper front rooms have good views of the Old Fort and the sea. It's in an old mansion that has been restored without losing the old-fashioned style. The rooms are a bit spartan but do have all mod cons.
✉ **Kapodistriou 4, Corfu Town** ☎ **0661 39041 fax 0661 39283**

Corfu Hilton (£££)
Luxury resort hotel close to the airport and a taxi (or bus) ride away from Corfu Town. Two restaurants, several bars, snack bars, two pools and a casino are among the facilities.
✉ **Nausícaa, Kanoní** ☎ **0661 36540 fax 0661 36540**

Lefkáda
Hotel Apollo (£)
A good find in the windsurfers' resort of Vassilikí, this hotel has a roof terrace, rooms overlooking the bay, friendly staff and – unusual for a hotel – a restaurant of a very high standard.
✉ **Vassilikí** ☎ **0645 31122 fax 0645 31142**

Paxoí
Paxos Beach Hotel (££)
As resort hotels go this is far more attractive than most, with stone buildings and simple guest rooms, all of which have patios looking out to the sea. The beach is pebble and there is a restaurant, if you don't want the short walk into Gáios Town.
✉ **Gáios** ☎ **0662 32211 fax 0662 32166**

Zákynthos
Stráda Marína (££)
Perfectly situated on the waterfront in the capital town, this smart hotel has all the modern amenities and a roof terrace with excellent views too.
✉ **Lomvárdou 14, Chóra** ☎ **0695 22761 fax 0695 28733**

Saronic & Northern Aegean Islands

Aígina

Eginitíko Archontíko (£)

This Traditional Hotel (as the name translates) has only 12 rooms, and they are simple but furnished in traditional style.

✉ Eakoú 1, Aígínia Town
☎ 0297 24968 fax 0297 26716

Chíos

Hotel Kyma (£)

Dating back to 1917, the rooms in this mansion have been thoroughly modernised and it offers great value for money.

✉ Evyeniás Handrí 1, Chíos Town ☎ 0271 44500 fax 0278 44600

Lésvos

Hotel Blue Sea (£)

If you need to overnight near the port, this modernised hotel has double-glazing to ensure a good night's sleep. There are 61 ensuite rooms, pleasant without being luxurious, and reasonably priced for the convenient location.

✉ Koundouriótou 91, Mytilíni
☎ 0251 23995 fax 0251 29656

Límnos

Hotel Lemnos (£)

Cheap hotel on the harbour but still clean, quiet and friendly; ideal if you have an early ferry to catch or a late arrival.

✉ Arvanitáki, Myrina ☎ 0254 22153 fax 0254 23494

Póros

Hotel Sirena (£/££)

Póros is not too well-served with good hotels, but this is the best on the island. Its 120 rooms are spacious, all are ensuite with air-conditioning and telephone, there is a beach nearby and

it is in a quiet spot. For all this the room rates are surprisingly reasonable.

✉ Monastíri, Askéli
☎ 0298 22741 fax 0298 22744

Sámos

Pension Avli (£)

For those who like the simple life this guesthouse in a former convent provides a unique place to stay. It even has a crypt – though not available to rent. Some of the rooms are not ensuite but the price reflects this, and the owner is very hospitable.

✉ Lykoúrgou, Sámos Town
☎ 0273 22939

Skópelos

Hotel Denise (£)

Great location looking down over the town, this hotel with its own pool seems to be under-priced. The only drawback seems to be that its popularity means it is booked well ahead.

✉ Skópelos Town ☎ 0424 22678 fax 0424 22769

Spétses

Hotel Possidónion (££)

Completely renovated a few years ago, without losing its classical appearance, the front rooms have great sea views.

✉ Dápia ☎ 0298 72006 fax 0298 72208

Ýdra

Hotel Bratsera (£££)

Swish new hotel close to the harbour in beautiful grounds – hard to tell it was once a sponge factory. The 23 rooms are all tastefully done out in local style, and there is a pool in the grounds.

✉ Tombázi, Ýdra Town
☎ 0298 53971 fax 0298 53626

Breakfast

Hotels charge per room, and if breakfast is served it will be added to the bill as a separate item. The cost of breakfast should be shown on the notice in your room indicating the room rate. In some cases it may be compulsory, but the hotel should make this clear to you when you book. Far too many hotels only serve a perfunctory breakfast of a few rolls and some instant coffee, so you may prefer to eat out.

Cyclades

Passports
Have your passport handy when checking into a hotel. The proprietors need your passport number and other details for the hotel register, so may ask to keep it for a day or so till the paperwork has been done. They will always let you have it back again if you need it to change travellers' cheques.

Mýkonos
Hotel Delphines (££)
Tiny (7-room) hotel in town centre which is basic – the price indicates how expensive the island is generally – but clean and friendly. All room are ensuite, and comparing cost with facilities, this is one of the best bets in the area.
✉ **Mavroyénous, Chóra**
☎ **0289 22292 fax 0289 27307**

Náxos
Chateau Zevgoli (£)
In a restored mansion between the harbour and the fortress, this small hotel of just 14 ensuite rooms offers a real bargain. Rooms all open off a central courtyard and each is uniquely designed and comfortable.
✉ **Chóra** ☎ **0285 22993 fax 0285 24525**

Páros
Astir of Páros (£££)
Páros's best hotel is almost a Cycladic village in its own right, with its own pool, gym, beach, tiny golf course and even an art gallery. The reception area also displays of modern Greek art, and though it's expensive it's worth the outlay.
✉ **Kolymbíthres Beach, near Náoussa** ☎ **0284 51797 fax 0284 51985**

Cyclades Hotel (££)
Situated on a quiet street that leads to Livadía beach, the hotel is also handy for the bus station and the harbour. The style of architecture is typically Cycladic; gardens and all rooms have phone, balcony and bathroom.
✉ **Parikía, Livadía** ☎ **0284 24859/22840**

Hotel Dina (£)
This is the kind of hotel it is hard to imagine existing anywhere else in the world – just 8 ensuite rooms, all wonderfully clean, central, yet cheap.
✉ **Parikía** ☎ **0284 21325**

Sífnos
Hotel Sífnos (£)
With only 9 rooms, all ensuite, this hotel books up quickly in season but is worth trying to get into or booking ahead.
✉ **Apollonía** ☎ **0284 31624**

Sýros
Hotel Omiros (££)
This elegant hotel in a pedestrianised street only just creeps into the more expensive bracket, and its quiet setting and large rooms make it well worth the price.
✉ **Omírou 43, Ermoúpolis** ☎ **0281 84910 fax 0281 86266**

Thíra
Loucas Hotel (££)
This long-established hotel has 20 ensuite rooms and overlooks the Caldera. The rooms are unique, having been designed like caves in case of earthquake, and sharing patios which have some of the best views in the Aegean.
✉ **Thíra Town** ☎ **0286 22480 fax 0286 24882**

Tínos
Hotel Eleana (£)
Very close to the harbour, this simple hotel has 17 ensuite rooms and is a real bargain if you want to spend a few days in the island capital, or just have an early ferry to catch.
✉ **Plateía Ierarchón, Tínos Town** ☎ **0283 22561**

Dodecanese

Kálymnos

Archondíko Hotel (£)

Beautiful old mansion converted into a 10-room family-run hotel. Rooms are all ensuite with telephones, and have the original high ceilings. Very friendly owners, who have retained some of the mansion's antique furniture to provide a comfortable atmosphere at very reasonable prices.

✉ Póthi ☎ 0243 24051 fax 0243 24149

Kárpathos

Amopí Beach (£)

Cheap and simple hotel but right on the beach and a wonderful place for a relaxing break.

✉ Ammopí Beach ☎ 0245 22723

Kós

Hotel Affendoúlis (£)

A bargain in a quiet street in the heart of Kós Town. There are only 17 rooms but all are ensuite and have balconies. The hotel is well run, and has a kitchen where you can help yourself to drinks and snacks, provided you note down what you have.

✉ Evrepílou 1, Kós Town ☎ 0242 25321 fax 0242 25797

Leipsoí

Calypso Hotel (£)

The Calypso can claim to be the best hotel in town: it's the only one, at present. It is close to the harbour so handy for ferries, and the rooms are clean and have balconies. Surprisingly cheap.

✉ Leipsoí Town ☎ 0247 41242 fax 0247 41242

Pátmos

Australis Hotel (£)

The grounds around this lovely hotel look like the Garden of Eden, and are reason enough for staying here. There are 21 ensuite rooms, and the owners will soon make you feel like you're one of the family.

✉ Skála ☎ 0247 31476

Ródos (Rhodes)

Hotel Kastro (£)

A very simple hotel in the heart of the Old Town, overlooking the Turkish Baths. To stay in such a setting at these prices is an incredible bargain.

✉ Arionos 14, Rhodes Old Town ☎ 0241 20446

S Nikolis Hotel (££)

An Old Town hotel which oozes history, incorporating stonework that goes back 800 years. The rooms are all modern, though, and the price, given the atmosphere, is reasonable.

✉ Ippodamou 61, Rhodes Old Town ☎ 0241 34561 fax 0241 32034

Sými

Aliki (£/££)

Long part of Sými life, the friendly Aliki has a prime spot overlooking the water, but around the corner from the busy harbour itself. Simple but comfortable.

✉ Yialós ☎ 0241 71665 fax 0241 71655

Tílos

Hotel Iríni (£)

Wonderful gardens tended by the owner's father surround this exceptional hotel, where visitors return year after year. Expertly run by the Ílias, whose Hawaiian outfits add to the colour.

✉ Livádia ☎ 0241 44293

Look First

No one will be surprised or offended if you ask to look at a room before booking it. Any decent hotel will be happy to show you what they have available. Don't be afraid to ask if they have anything better, as they may show you the nearest rather than the best room available.

Ionian Islands

Haggling

Haggling is not as common a custom in the Greek Islands as it is further to the east and the south of the Mediterranean. However, a bit of bargaining may be called for if you're buying in an antique shop, or are considering buying more than one item. Lots of shops in tourist towns have inflated prices, and where any aggressive selling goes on, such as the streets of the Old Town on Rhodes, then a bit of aggressive buying is also called for.

Arts and Handicrafts

Alexander's

Large and varied collection of Greek handicrafts including jewellery hand-made by the shop's owner, plus ceramics, dolls in island costumes, embroidery and unusual hand-made glass items.

✉ **Vergóti, Argostóli, Kefalloniá** ☎ **0671 23057**

Bizarre

Corfu Town is good for clothes shopping, from cheap and cheerful (and cheeky) T-shirts to more upmarket designer labels. Bizarre has more outrageous designs mainly from Greece but some from Asia too.

✉ **Arseníou 27, Corfu Town** ☎ **0661 26384**

Danília Village

This attempt at reconstructing a 200-year-old Greek village shows displays of people at work, tilling fields and so on, but also it includes artisans whose work is for sale.

✉ **Near Goúvia, Kérkyra** ☎ **0661 36833**

Elli

An outlet for the hand-embroidered tablecloths and other items produced by the island women. Good quality work is expensive but the shop's owner will explain how many months of work go into some items. Smaller items are also for sale, all exquisitely made.

✉ **Theotóki 88, Corfu Town** ☎ **0661 26283**

Gentilini Vineyard

This small-scale vineyard does not do organised tours so telephone before visiting.

If it is convenient you will get a personal tour of the vineyard and a chance to sample and buy some of the very high quality wine.

✉ **Miniés, Kefalloniá** ☎ **0671 41618**

Handicraft Cooperative

On the waterfront, by the harbour, is this excellent shop selling a range of island-made products, including rugs, clothing, embroidery and tablecloths.

✉ **Lombárdou 42, Zákynthos Town** ☎ **n/a**

Olive Wood Workshop

Corfu has a long tradition of olive wood carving, and this is one of several small workshops in the Old Town's winding back streets where you can watch the craftsmen at work. The resulting salad and fruit bowls, serving spoons and vases all make elegant souvenirs.

✉ **Theotóki 131, Corfu Town** ☎ **0661 47375**

Vassilakis

One of the largest stocks of Greek wines, spirits and liqueurs that you will find anywhere in the Greek Islands, with tastings before you buy.

✉ **Opposite Achillion Palace, Kérkyra** ☎ **0661 52440**

Terracotta

Good quality outlet for arts and craft items made only by Greek artists. These are excellent examples of work, such as sculptures and ceramics, which may be expensive but is of the best quality.

✉ **Filarmonikís 2, Corfu Town** ☎ **0661 45260**

Saronic & Northern Aegean Islands

Archipelago
These two interesting shops have a mix of antiques, unusual arts and craft items and clothing, well worth browsing through
✉ **Skíathos Town and Skópelos Town**
☎ **0427 22163 and 0424 23127**

Aris
For a good selection of bright and cheerful clothing, which includes some hand-painted shirts and T-shirts.
✉ **Agliánous 4, Skíathos Town**
☎ **0427 22415**

The Art Cooperative
This is a really delightful little shop which helps the women of the area find an outlet for their work, specifically the wonderful hand-made dolls wearing traditional island costumes. They make unique gifts and are a refreshing change from much of the tourist tat.
✉ **Kallimásia Village, Chíos**
☎ **0271 51180**

Athens School of Fine Arts
This highly regarded art school has occasional exhibitions of its students' work, with the chance to buy something original and at the same time help a young artist.
✉ **Krallis Mansion, Mólyvos, Lésvos** ☎ **n/a**

Eleftéris Diakoyiánnis
A good selection of ceramics, not just from Aígina but from all over the Greek Islands, and the mainland too. Also has a selection of jewellery, and reproductions of Greek sculpture.
✉ **Demokratías 39, Aígina Town** ☎ **0297 24593**

Faltaits Museum
Small museum of Folk Art has a workshop and shop attached where you can buy the work of modern craftsmen and women, keeping the island traditions alive. The museum also has an outlet, called Argo, on the main street.
✉ **Skýros Town** ☎ **Museum: 0222 91232; Argo: 0222 92158**

Galerie Varsakis
Owned by an artist whose surreal paintings are also for sale, this arts and crafts treasure trove includes jewellery, embroidery, carvings and carpets, as well as a number of interesting antiques.
✉ **Plateía Trion Ierárchon, Skíathos Town** ☎ **0427 22255**

Hermes
Ýdra Town is as good as any in the Greek Islands for shopping for arts and crafts, though the prices can be high. This shop has a particularly good array of jewellery.
✉ **Harbour, Ýdra Town**
☎ **0298 52689**

Island
A good quality clothes shop stocking a wide range of Greek-made cotton T-shirts as well as other casual clothing.
✉ **Papadiamádis, Skíathos Town** ☎ **0427 23377**

Stamatis Ftoulis
A retail outlet for traditional-style island ceramics, made at the owner's workshop at Magazía. There is a good range of tasteful hand-painted plates, bowls, vases and other items.
✉ **Skýros Town** ☎ **0222 91559**

What to Buy
Most of the islands have good distinctive ceramics, and nothing conjures up a picture of Greece as well as a piece of white and bright blue pottery. Carpets and *kilims* also make good buys, and there is a lot of good-quality hand-made jewellery, particularly using turquoise and silver. Local produce is also worth seeking out: honey, cheese, herbs and spices.

Cyclades

Opening Hours

Most shops open every morning from Monday to Saturday, sometimes from very early through to about 1-2PM. They will then close for a few hours for an afternoon siesta, and re-open at about 5-7PM. Many then stay open quite late, or as long as there are customers around. In busy tourist areas, and in the summer, souvenir shops will often stay open all day, including weekends, whereas ordinary shops such as supermarkets may well close on Saturday afternoon and all day Sunday.

Batsi Gold

Good collection of jewellery inspired by ancient Greek myths and legends: bracelets, ear-rings, necklaces, brooches, rings.

✉ Batsi, Ándr0s ☎ 0282 41575

Canava Roussos

They make some good wine on Santoríni and here is a chance to sample at source, and buy a few bottles at prices lower than you will pay in the shops.

✉ Between Thíra and Kamári ☎ 0286 31278

Centre for Contemporary Art

You could shop till you drop in Mýkonos, as the gay scene has produced a great number of tasteful arts, crafts and clothing shops, responding to the demand. This centre concentrates on current Greek artists, giving you an idea of what's happening in the modern Greek art scene.

✉ Koúzi Yorgoúli 43 ☎ 0289 26868

Harris Prassas Ostria-Tinos

This jeweller has produced an eclectic collection of work, incorporating ancient and modern styles, in both silver and gold. Much of it has a religious theme, given Tínos's place as a pilgrimage site.

✉ Evangelístrias 20, Tínos Town ☎ 0283 23893

Hersónissos

Craft shop with a good range of modern jewellery and pottery, in an area where there are several others of this type.

✉ Apollonía, Sífnos ☎ 0284 32209

Ilias Lalaounis

The most famous jeweller in Greece, who even has his own museum in Athens, has an outlet here. His work has been inspired by all kinds of things – Celtic myths, Greek legends, Byzantine art – and is often superb, but expensive.

✉ Polykandrióti 14, Mýkonos Town ☎ 0289 22444

Antonis Kalogirou

This potter sells his own distinctive style, in Sífnos style, and also sells paintings of island life which are much better than many of the mass-produced prints on sale everywhere.

✉ Harbour, Kamáres, Sífnos ☎ 0284 31651

Paraporti

Craft items, especially ceramics, from Ándros. Also embroidery, some jewellery and model ships.

✉ Plateía Kairís, Ándros Town ☎ 0282 23777

Studio Yría

If you want to buy something modern but made from the superb quality Parian marble, head for this artists' studio where a husband and wife team produce some fine examples. They also have distinctive island ceramics, embroidery and metalwork too.

✉ Kóstos Village, Páros ☎ 0284 29007

Tirokomiká Proïónia Náxou

Fantastic food and drink shop, an essential visit if you want to take anything home or simply prepare a fine picnic with local cheeses, all kinds of olives, local wines.

✉ Papavasilíou, Náxos Town ☎ 0285 22230

Dodecanese

Katoí
There is a good choice of jewellery, icons and especially ceramics of the island.
✉ **Chóra, Pátmos** ☎ **0247 31487**

Rhodes
Rhodes is easily the best island in the Dodecanese for shopping. Not only is it prosperous, it is also a regular port of call for cruise ships in the Aegean. The shops cater for wealthy visitors – prices can be high and you need to watch for overcharging – but there is a good range of fur, jewellery and leather shops in the New Town, and many in the Old Town too. Don't neglect the side streets running off the main shopping street of Sokrátous, where you will find a number of more specialist shops, such as jewellers and antique dealers. Especially good is Panetiou, opposite the entrance to the Palace of the Grand Masters, with several unusual antique, craft and fashion shops.

Museum Reproduction Shop
The Greek Ministry of Culture authorises the faithful reproduction of many of the finest antiquities in its collections. A good source of these excellent replicas is this shop in the Old Town of Rhodes, just beyond the Archaeological Museum, at the foot of Ippodon.
✉ **Ippotón, Old Town, Rhodes** ☎ **Daily 8AM–8PM**

Traditional Art Shop
In among the dozens of identical souvenir shops in the Old Town of Rhodes is this much more original one. It stocks unusual pottery, icons, and many examples of Greek arts and crafts.
✉ **Ippodamou 40-42** ☎ **0241 38431**

Sponges
Many shops sell sponges, and almost all tourist shops will have at least a few on display. To know what you're buying, though, you should first visit one of the centres listed below. They'll explain what to look for in a good sponge, and allow you to test several types. Remember, naturally coloured brown sponges are stronger than artificially coloured, yellow ones; smaller holes make better sponges and cut sponges do not last as long as whole sponges.

Aegean Sponge Centre
Thousand of sponges for sale on an island which once made part of its wealth from sponge-fishing. The owners will demonstrate how to tell quality sponges, and talk about the life of the sponge-fishermen.
✉ **Harbour, Sými** ☎ **n/a**

Astor Workshop of Sea Sponges
See the whole process of sponge production on the island that's known for it throughout Greece. And, of course, a chance to buy some of the best quality sponges.
✉ **Póthia, Kálymnos** ☎ **0243 29815**

Exporting Antiquities
It is illegal to export antiquities, including icons, from Greece, although there is no problem of course with modern copies. Occasionally someone may whisper to you that they have a genuine antique for sale, showing you perhaps a piece of a statue or a battered icon. If it is genuine then you are breaking the law by buying it, and will be severely dealt with either by Greek customs or your own customs officials if it is found. If it is not genuine then you are being cheated. The simple solution is not to have anything to do with it.

Places of Interest for Children

Swimming

Greek children learn to swim at an early age and are very at home in the water. However, their natural inclination to show off can lead to them doing things – backflips and so on – that your children may not be able to emulate, but may try to, so keep an eye on them. The only real dangers in the water are occasional problems with sea urchins and jellyfish. Always wearing shoes if there are rocks nearby, where urchins may live, can help.

The beach is the main focus for most family holidays in the Greek Islands. The sea is generally warm and, in the sheltered bays, shallow enough for even young children to swim safely. In many resorts, the watersports offered will be suitable for older children.

On a Ferry

Most children love ferry rides, and a short hop from one island to the next is guaranteed to be an adventure. Let them watch for dolphins or flying fish (which they are far more likely to see). Take care with the sun, as it is very easy to get burned when the cooling sea breezes take away the full impact of the sun.

Take a Bus

A bus ride to another island town, or to a deserted beach, is another form of adventure. Although there are fixed stops, Greek buses will stop wherever there is someone to pick up or put down, so asking the children to wave down the bus will appeal.

Eating Out

Greek children eat out with their families so let your children join in too. Waiters will probably make a fuss of them, and it has been known for children to disappear into the kitchen where the staff will act as unofficial babysitters while the parents enjoy a break.

Greek Children

Most towns and villages have somewhere where the children gather to play in the evenings, probably in sight of their parents who may be sitting having a coffee or a glass of *ouzo*. Let your children join in. Children need a common language much less than adults do, and they will be perfectly safe. Greece is one of the safest countries in the world.

Ionian Islands

Fortresses

In Corfu Town visit the Old Fortress and the New Fortress, with battlements to explore, dungeons to visit and views to enjoy. Elsewhere on the island there are fortresses too, at Paleokastrítsa, for example. Throughout these islands there are Venetian fortresses, most of them open to the public and sometimes free of charge.

Turtles

On Zákynthos there are boat rides out to try to see the endangered loggerhead turtles which live in the waters off Laganás. As well as being educational, it reminds locals that the turtles are an attraction in their own right.

Caves

The Blue Caves at the northern end of Zákynthos can be entered on a boat trip, and on Kefalloniá you may want to take children in to see the Drogaráti cave and the Melisánni Cave, which you visit by boat. Both of these are near Sámi. The former is a huge cavern with impressive stalactites and stalagmites. The latter is very different; filled with water and open to the sky where the roof has fallen in.

Saronic and Northern Aegean Islands

On Lésvos the castle at Mólyvos is well worth exploring,especially if combined with a visit to the little harbour where there will be activity around the fishing boats at certain times of the day.

The Hellenic Wildlife Hospital on Aígina looks after rescued, injured animals and re-introduces them to the wild. It is not open to the public but anyone with a special interest will be shown around ☎ 0297 22882.

On Skíathos boat trips to many of the island's caves can be arranged from most resorts.

Cyclades

On Thíra a boat trip out into the Caldera should entertain children, if the guide has some suitably dramatic tales of the volcanic eruption that happened here to create the island as it stands.

Dodecanese

In Rhodes Town, on Rhodes, there is an aquarium, with the rather grand and misleading official title 'Hydrobiological Institute'. Don't be put off, it still is a regular aquarium, with large glass tanks showing off the local sea life. On the same island, children will enjoy visiting the Valley of the Butterflies (► 89).

On Nísyros, a visit to the volcano's crater (► 86) is sure to be enjoyable – if a little hot.

Athens

Travelling to the islands often involves spending a night in Athens and you may wish to spend a little time exploring the Greek capital as part of your holiday.

The Hellenic Children's Museum

There are interactive displays, such as one on the new metro being built under Athens, and computers to play on, and rooms full of art materials to enjoy. Some of the staff speak English and they welcome children of all ages and nationalities, but advance notice for visits by non-Greek speaking children is advisable.
- ✉ **Kidathineon 14**
- ☎ **01 331 2995**
- 🕐 **Fri-Mon and Wed 10AM–5PM**
Closed public holidays.

The Museum of Greek Children's Art

A small and lively museum, displaying the work of schoolchildren from all over Greece, including imaginative sculptures. There are also materials for children to use.
- ✉ **Kodrou 9**
- ☎ **01 331 2621**
- 🕐 **Tue-Sat 10AM–2PM, Sun 11AM–2PM**
Closed public holidays

The Aquarium

Worth knowing about if there are unexpected flight delays or long waits at the airport. There are several tanks of exotic fish and a crocodile named Kosmos. A short taxi ride will get you to it from outside the airport.
- ✉ **Agios Kosmos Sports Area**
- ☎ **01 894 5640**
- 🕐 **Mon-Fri 10AM–3PM**

Ruins

Taking children to see an archaeological site may not be the most obvious choice, but in many places there are theatres and running tracks, where children can play while their parents soak up the more historical atmosphere.

Entertainment &
Nightlife

Cover Charge
Some clubs and discos
have a free entry policy
until a certain time, and
then introduce a cover
charge, while in others you
will pay an entry fee no
matter what time you turn
up. The cover usually
includes one drink, but it's
not always the drink of
your choice. You'll be
given a voucher which the
barman will exchange for
maybe a glass of cheap
wine. Drink prices are then
high, but that's the cost of
a good time.

Most people's evening
entertainment in the Greek
Islands is a stroll around
followed by an *ouzo*, a
lengthy meal and perhaps a
brandy or cup of coffee in a
café afterwards. Even the
smallest resorts usually run
to at least one disco, but
these can range from the
ultra-modern with sound
shows to the more rural
level. The author has fond
memories of being in a disco
on one island when a family
of ducks waddled in through
the entrance and across the
dance floor.

Ionian Islands
Corfu is still the place to
head for if your holiday is to
include late-night music and
bars. Benítses and Kávos are
the two main resorts, with
Future in Kávos being the
number one club. In Corfu
Town there is an 11PM
curfew on loud music within
the town's boundaries, so
the action is slightly further
out. The 'disco strip' runs
north along the coast
towards Kondokáli, and the
biggest disco, with its own
swimming pool and huge
video displays, is the
Hippodrome (☎ 0661
43150). Other favourites are
Coca Flash and Apokalypsis
(with an Olympic flame on
the roof). The scene changes
constantly, though, so get
up-to-date with a copy of one
of the local English-language
newspapers, such as *The
Corfiot*.

If you have more
sophisticated tastes then
there is a Casino in the
Achilleion Palace (☎ 0661
56210) in the summer. The
cafés along the Liston are

where locals like to sit to
watch the world go by and
see the night out with a
glass of brandy. The Old
Fortress is the location for
Sound and Light shows
several times a week in
various languages in the
summer months.

Zákynthos is the next
choice for a good night life,
and in Zákynthos Town, The
Base is the place, a bar on
Plateía Áyiou Márkou where
the drink and dance crowd
hang out, and San Marco,
which favours British disco
music. The main discos near
town are to the south in
Argási, one of the main
resorts, with Laganás
running it close and having
dozens of bars and clubs to
choose from.

There is a big enough tourist
industry on **Kefalloniá** to
warrant good nightlife in the
main resorts. In the capital,
Argostóli, the central Plateía
Metaxá has several bars
playing music. The main
resorts for late-night action
are Lassí and Póros, and
even the elegant-looking
Fiskárdo on the northern tip
has bars open well into the
night.

On **Lefkáda**, the liveliest and
noisiest resorts are Nydrí, on
the east coast, where bars
blare out music till the early
hours, and Vassilikí in the
south, where the
windsurfers know how to
have a good time. Zeus' Bar
is where the Godlike and
sometimes not-so-Godlike
bodies parade themselves at
night.

On little **Paxoí** and **Itháki**,

nightlife revolves around the cafés and handful of bars, and the same on **Kýthera** where the visitors are mainly Greek.

Saronic and Northern Aegean Islands

The **Saronic Islands**, attracting the Athenians, tend to be busy at weekends and there is no shortage of things to do in the evening. The clubs and discos tend to be less sophisticated than you get in the resorts which attract young European travellers, but the Athenians are just as determined to enjoy themselves. Don't rent a room over a late-night bar if you're not prepared to join in the fun yourself.

On **Aígina** the Iris Club is popular, as is the Eltiana nightclub behind Avra Beach. Across the island in the resort of Ágia Marína there are more clubs and discos than in Aígina Town itself. There are also a couple of summer cinemas, and another is on the island of Póros: the Diana Open-Air Cinema. Popular bars on Póros are the Korali and the Sirocco. On Ýdra the clubs are a bit more sophisticated and a lot more expensive. Disco Heaven is a good bet, and underneath here is Saronicos, with Greek music and late-night revelry. On Spétses you can get blasted at Club Fever, every Wednesday, Friday and Sunday from 11PM, as the 3000dr cover charge provides you with all the drink you can down.

In the Sporades, **Skíathos** is the island for hedonists, with the main town packed with pubs and clubs, centred around the streets of Politékniou, Evangelístra and Papadiamántis. **Skópelos** isn't yet quite as frantic, but there are enough music places in the main town to keep fans happy. They tend to be jazz rather than disco, though, such as the Platános Jazz Club close to the pier. For Greek music and partying try Anö Kato or one of the other clubs behind Plateía Platános.

Dodecanese

Rhodes and **Kós** are the two main party islands, but Rhodes is big enough to encompass plenty of culture too. In the Old Town on Androníkou is the Folk Dance Theatre (☎ 0241 29085), with evening shows on Monday, Wednesday and Friday throughout the summer months. There is also a Sound and Light Show (☎ 0241 36795) next to the Old Town, near the main taxi rank, in different languages on different nights. There are also some bars and clubs within the Old Town, which tend to be more sophisticated than the revelry that takes place outside. Try the Theater Bar or the Grand Master's Inn for pleasant atmosphere.

Rhodes claims to have more discos per capita than any of the world's major cities, and there are plenty of these in Rhodes New Town. Orfanídou Street has gained the nickname of Bar Street, so if you start the night there you won't go far wrong. All the resorts down the east

What's On?

Bars and clubs open and close with greater frequency than tavernas, and what's fashionable one year may be closed the next or the owners have opened a new club elsewhere. To keep in touch with what's happening, it's worth looking out for any local papers or magazines that are aimed at the visitors, with ads and reviews of the current scene. Most busy islands have them, usually in English and occasionally in German, and you should be able to find them in kiosks, book and stationery shops, and some souvenir shops where paperbacks and magazines are also sold.

Staying Legal

It is neither polite nor wise to make discourteous public comments about the Greek religion, culture or the state. Such action may be judged as an offence and treated as such by the police. Recreational drug use and especially supplying drugs of any kind, is considered a major crime. Supplying even small amounts of drugs may result in a very long prison sentence, even life. If you are arrested in any circumstances, you have the right to contact your consulate.

and west coasts close to Rhodes Town have plenty of night-time entertainment of their own.

Kós Town is also a party town, and the bars and clubs are concentrated in two main districts. The first is around Porfíriou, close to the beach on the north end of town, and here are names like the Crazy Horse Saloon and the Fashion Club. The second area is Exarhía, the name of the district around Pávlou and Koundouriótou, where Saloon Tex is packed every night, through till the early hours. In either case, after about 9PM, just follow the noise.

Cyclades

All the island groups have one or two islands where night-time entertainment is high on the agenda, but the Cyclades has three of them: **Mýkonos**, **Íos** and **Thíra**. All have their different styles, though. Thíra is for the more sophisticated party animal, prepared to pay the higher prices for a touch more chic. Mýkonos is also sophisticated but has traditionally appealed to the gay crowd, though this is less so these days. The nightlife there tends to be sophisticated but raunchy. Íos is simply party island, without too much sophistication.

Mýkonos Town has a bar or club to suit every taste, even Greek, somewhat surprisingly. The Mýkonos Bar, by the waterfront in the area known as Little Venice, has Greek dancers who demonstrate their own

talents and then everyone joins in, till they stagger out in the early hours. The bar doesn't even open until 10PM. Next to it is the Caprice, which opens earlier but stays open just as late. If you like a bit of variety then try the Skandinavian Bar, also near the waterfront. It's a complex which spreads over two buildings, so there's a choice of bars and music, and again it goes on till the early hours.

Íos is such a party island that things hardly seem to start till the early hours. Many of the town's 100-plus bars have happy hours earlier in the evening, and then as midnight approaches the partying takes off. Most of the bars are packed into the maze of back streets that make up the old village area, but anything less like an old Greek village is hard to imagine. You can even buy Irish Guinness on draught in the Dubliner Bar, while the nearby Sweet Irish Dream has no entry charge before 2AM, and is where most people seem to end up as dawn approaches. The Slammer Bar specialises in Tequila Slammers, not surprisingly, while another popular spot is the Scorpion Disco, on the edge of town. If you want to party Greek-style then Anemos has Greek music and dancing.

Thíra means 'wild island', but it has never been as wild as it is today, with bars, clubs and discos making sure that there's never a quiet moment on a midsummer evening. There are no prizes for guessing who hangs out in the Backpacker Bar, but it does at least mean that the drinks are cheaper than in the smarter places. The Tithora Club in the main square of Thíra Town opens at 10PM and features heavy rock till 4AM, while for those who want jazz and an early night the Kira Thíra Jazz Club closes at 3AM. Next door is the Trip into the Music, for dance fans, as are the Koo Club and Enigma.

Compared to these three islands, the others in the Cyclades are mere novices, but **Páros** is busy enough to have a good night scene, mainly on the waterfront in Páros Town, while **Náxos** Town has a few discos and clubs where you'll have no trouble dancing till the middle of the night.

Sport

In the islands sport means mainly watersports. There is one golf course, on Corfu, but elsewhere conditions are too hot and dry to maintain golf greens. Many of the larger islands have their own football and basketball teams, as both these sports are huge in Greece, and you might be lucky and coincide with an inter-island match to watch.

Tennis is quite popular though there are few public courts. Most courts are in the resort hotels, but they may allow non-residents to use them during quiet periods.

Corfu has a cricketing tradition which dates back to the island's status as a

British Protectorate in the 19th century. These days it is an essential part of the summer scene, down on the Esplanade. British clubs often tour there and the Corfu team has represented Greece in international competition.

But aside from walking and cycling, if you want to get some sporting exercise it will be by the water. Almost every popular beach will have at least one, usually several, watersports operations. These range from simply hiring out pedaloes or windsurfers to giving tuition in water-skiing, windsurfing and scuba-diving (▶ 81 'In the Know'). Underwater photography requires a special permit (it's not a good idea to dive in working harbours or near busy anchorages). Parascending is now widely popular on the main beaches, though check your holiday insurance before you indulge. Most watersports are cheap by Mediterranean standards, so take the opportunity to try out something new.

The Movies

Open-air cinema is popular throughout Greece, and in the islands in the summer temporary outdoor cinemas are sometimes set up. They are aimed at locals not visitors, but even so, many do show foreign films in the original language, with Greek subtitles. Don't expect too much reverence for the work of the director. It's common practice to wander round, talk to your friends and shout out comments.

Protection

If you feel you have been cheated, do report a place to the Tourist Police. Even if it is not possible to prove anything, it may discourage the staff from trying it again. The Police may overlook one incident, but if they are continually called to a place they will start to get annoyed, and they do have the power to revoke a club's licence.

What's On When

Name Days

Greek adults celebrate name days rather than birthdays, that is to say the feast day of the Saint after whom they are named. In many places this means, for example, that on 24 June, the Feast of St John the Baptist, all men named Ioánnis will get together and organise a meal or a party, often inviting everyone, locals and visitors alike. Visitors might be asked to make a small contribution to the cost of the food and wine, but a good time is guaranteed.

January

1 January: Feast of St Basil.
6 January: The Epiphany. On many islands 'Blessings of the Waters' take place.

February-March

Clean Monday (Katharí Deftéri): On the last Monday before Lent, marks the end of a carnival period and the beginning of Lent.
25 March: Independence Day, celebrating the revolt against the Turks. Major feasts on Tínos and Ýdra.

April

23 April: Feast of St George, with horse-racing on Límnos and Kós.

May

1 May: May Day, and traditional workers' parades.
21 May: Unification of the Ionian Islands with the rest of Greece, celebrated especially on Corfu.

June-July

Late June: Navy Week celebrated on many islands.
July: Cricket Week on Corfu.

August

15 August: The Feast of the Assumption. Tínos is the main place of pilgrimage.

October

28 October: Óchi Day, when General Metaxas allegedly gave a one-word response of Óchi (No) to Mussolini's request that his troops be allowed to pass through Greece.

December

The Greek year winds down with Christmas and New Year's Eve, neither are as important as Easter.

Moveable Feasts

Carnival (Karnaváli)

Carnival is not celebrated as widely – or wildly - in the Greek Islands as elsewhere in the world, but the Goat Dance of Skyros is a long-standing traditional Carnival event, and other islands do have festivities, notably the Ionians. These take place during the three weeks prior to Lent, with the biggest celebrations on the Sunday immediately before the start of Lent: seven weeks before Easter weekend.

Easter

Easter is the biggest event in the Greek year. The bier on which Christ's body will be laid is decorated with flowers, and on Good Friday evening is carried through the streets.

On Easter Saturday the main church service takes place, climaxing at midnight. On Easter Sunday Greek families get together for elaborate celebrations. It is a wonderful time to be in the Greek Islands because, although it signals the start of the tourist season, there are still relatively few visitors around. The date of Greek Easter occasionally coincides with Easter in the western calendar, but is usually a few weeks earlier or later, so always check if you wish to visit Greece at this time.

Whit

Seven weeks after Greek Easter, Whit Sunday and Monday are also celebrated across the Greek Islands. Monday is a national holiday with parades and parties.

Practical Matters

Above: *Dhiafani on Kárpathos*
Right: *taverna owner*

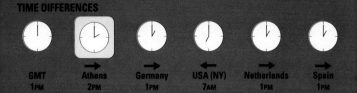

TIME DIFFERENCES

GMT	Athens	Germany	USA (NY)	Netherlands	Spain
1PM	2PM	1PM	7AM	1PM	1PM

BEFORE YOU GO

WHAT YOU NEED

- ● Required
- ○ Suggested
- ▲ Not required

	UK	Germany	USA	Netherlands	Spain
Passport/National Identity Card	●	●	●	●	●
Visa	▲	▲	▲	▲	▲
Onward or Return Ticket	▲	▲	▲	▲	▲
Health Inoculations (tetanus and polio)	▲	▲	▲	▲	▲
Health Documentation (reciprocal agreement ➤ 123, Health)	●	●	●	●	●
Travel Insurance	○	○	○	○	○
Driving Licence (National or International)	●	●	●	●	●
Car Insurance Certificate (if own car)	●	●	●	●	●
Car Registration Document (if own car)	●	●	●	●	●

WHEN TO GO

Greek Islands

High season

Low season

9°C	11°C	12°C	16°C	20°C	24°C	27°C	28°C	24°C	20°C	15°C	14°C
JAN	FEB	MAR	APR	MAY	JUN	JUL	AUG	SEP	OCT	NOV	DEC

🌧 Very wet 🌧 Wet ☁ Cloud ☀ Sun

TOURIST OFFICES

In the UK
The National Tourist
Organisation of Greece
(NTOG)
4 Conduit Street
London
W1R 0DJ
☎ 020 7734 5997
Fax: 020 7287 1369

In the USA
The National Tourist
Organisation of Greece
645 Fifth Avenue
New York
NY 10022
☎ (212)421-5777
Fax: (212) 826-6940

611 West Sixth Street
Suite 2198
Los Angeles
CA 92668
☎ (213)626-6696
Fax: (213) 489-9744

POLICE	100
FIRE	199
AMBULANCE	166
RED CROSS	150

WHEN YOU ARE THERE

ARRIVING

Most major airlines operate scheduled flights to Athens's Ellinikón International Airport. Other possible mainland airports are Thessaloníki (for the northern Aegean) and Préveza (for the Ionian Islands). Several isands also have their own airport, served by direct charter flights in summer (▶ 121).

Ellinikon Airport
Distance to Athens centre

10 kilometres

Journey times	
🚇	N/A
🚌	30 minutes
🚕	15 minutes

Port of Piréas
Distance to Athens centre

10 kilometres

Journey times	
🚇	N/A
🚌	60 minutes
🚕	15 minutes

MONEY

Greece's currency is the drachma, issued in notes of 100, 200, 500, 1,000, 5,000 and 10,000 drachma, and coins of 5, 10, 20, 50, 100 and 200 drachma. There may still be a few smaller drachma coins in circulation (and the blue 50 drachma note), but bills are generally rounded up or down to the nearest 5 drachma. Travellers' cheques are accepted by most hotels, shops and restaurants in lieu of cash, although the rate of exchange may be less favourable than in banks. Travellers' cheques in sterling or US dollars are the most convenient. There are countless banks in most major towns, and money exchange offices in smaller resorts, where travellers' cheques, cash and Eurocheques can be exchanged and advances on credit cards obtained.

TIME

Greece is two hours ahead of Greenwich Mean Time (GMT+2), and adjusts to summer time at 4AM on the last Sunday in March until 4AM on the last Sunday in October.

CUSTOMS

→ **YES**

Goods Obtained Duty Free outside the EU (Limits):
Alcohol (over 22% vol): 1L or Alcohol (not over 22% vol): 2L and
Still table wine: 2L,
Cigarettes: 200 or Cigars: 50 or Tobacco: 250gms
Perfume: 60ml
Toilet water: 250ml

Goods Bought Duty and Tax Paid for own use inside the EU (Guidance Levels):
Alcohol (over 22% vol): 10L
Alcohol (not over 22% vol): 20L and Wine (max 60L sparkling): 90L, Beer: 110L
Cigarettes: 800, Cigars: 200, Tobacco: 1kg
Perfume and toilet water: no limit
Visitors must be 17 or over to benefit from tobacco and alcohol allowances.

⊖ **NO**

Drugs, firearms, ammunition, offensive weapons, obscene material, unlicensed animals.

EMBASSIES AND CONSULATES

UK
723 6211

Germany
728 5111

USA
(01) 721 2951

Netherlands
723 9701

Spain
721 4885

WHEN YOU ARE THERE

TOURIST OFFICES

**Ellínikos Organismos
Tourísmou (EOT)**
(National Tourist
Organisation of Greece)

● PO Box 1017
Odós Amerikis 2
10564 Athens
☎ 01 322 3111
Fax: 01 325 2895

There is an information desk
at the Athens airport East
Terminal (01 969 4500) and
at Marina Zeas in Piréas
(☎ 01 428 4100).

Other EOT offices in the
islands are on Kefalloniá
(Customs Pier, Argostóli
☎ 0671 22248); Corfu
(corner of Vouleftón and
Mantzároun, Corfu Town
☎ 0661 37520); Lésvos
(Aristárkhou 6, Mytilíni ☎
1251 42511); Rhodes (Plateía
Rimínis, Rhodes Town
☎ 0241 35945); Sámos
(Martíou 25, Vathí ☎ 0273
28582).

NATIONAL HOLIDAYS

J	F	M	A	M	J	J	A	S	O	N	D
2	1	2		2	1		1		1		2

1 Jan	New Year's Day
6 Jan	Epiphany
25 March	Independence Day
Feb/Mar	Shrove Monday (41 days pre-Easter)
May/Jun Whit Monday	(50 days after Easter)
1 May	Labour Day
15 Aug	Assumption of the Virgin
28 Oct	Óchi Day
25 Dec	Christmas Day
26 Dec	St Stephen's Day

Restaurants and tourist shops may well stay open on
these days, but museums will be closed.

OPENING HOURS

○ Shops   ● Post Offices
● Offices   ◐ Attractions/museums
● Banks   ● Pharmacies

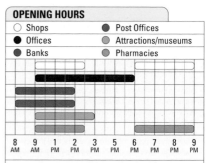

8 AM	9 AM	1 PM	2 PM	3 PM	5 PM	6 PM	7 PM	8 PM	9 PM

Shops in busy resorts will often stay open all hours in
the holiday season. Pharmacies are normally open on
weekdays only, but some open on Saturdays and
each one will always display details of the nearest
24-hour pharmacy. Monasteries usually open during
daylight hours, if no exact opening time is given.
Churches are often open all day, though some may
open early morning and evenings only. Opening hours
in Greece are very flexible, especially those of
museums, which often change. Longer hours operate
in summer (given in the guide), so if travelling
between October and Easter, check.

**DRIVE ON THE
RIGHT**

**TOILETS
BASIC**

★★
★★

PUBLIC TRANSPORT

 Internal Flights Islands that have their own airports are Corfu, Kefalloniá, Kós, Crete, Lésvos, Páros, Rhodes, Sámos, Skiáthos and Zákynthos. These offer not only charter flights in summer but also internal flights. The main airline is Olympic, but there are others, such as Air Greece and Chronos, so shop around. Most flights operate to and from Athens, but there are some flights direct from island to island. They are not generally expensive.

 Buses Greece generally has a very good and cheap bus service, and this extends to most islands. Buses will often meet ferries to take people to the resort towns. Even the smallest islands generally have some kind of bus service: look for timetables at bus stops, in the main square or simply ask in a shop or bar.

 Ferries There is an extensive network of ferries linking the Greek islands with each other, with the mainland (particularly Athens) and with some other Mediterranean countries, notably Italy. Services are much more frequent in summer, and there is an increasing number of fast hydrofoil services. See the individual island entries for the main ferry connections. Note that different companies operate different boats, and competition is fierce. Any one ticket office will only give you details of its own ferries and even deny the existence of other ferries that might be more convenient for you. Ask in several places to be sure.

 Trains There are no railway services on any of the islands.

CAR RENTAL

 Most leading car rental companies have offices in the main island towns and at airport terminals, and even smaller resorts will probably have a few local hire firms. Car hire in Greece is expensive, however, and accident rates are high.

TAXIS

 Taxis are cheap compared with other countries, and are metered. Drivers may stop to pick up other passengers going in the same direction, each paying their share of the fare when they leave. Book ahead if the journey is important.

DRIVING

 Speed limit on motorways: **120kph**

 Speed limit on main roads: **90kph**

 Speed limit on minor roads: **50kph**

 Must be worn in front seats and in rear seats where fitted. Children under 10 not allowed in front seats.

 80 micrograms of alcohol in 100ml of breath is a criminal offence, and from 50 to 80 micrograms a civil offence. Penalties in both cases are severe.

Petrol (*venzini*) is usually available in five grades: super (*sooper*), regular (*aplí*), unleaded (*amolyvdhi*), super unleaded (*sooper amolyvdhi*), and, confusingly, *petrelaio*, which is diesel. Petrol stations are normally open 7–7 (closed Sun); larger ones (often self-service) are open 24 hours. Most take credit cards. There are few petrol stations in remote areas, but many islands have maps that mark them.

If you break down driving your own car then the Automobile and Touring Club of Greece (ELPA) provide 24-hour road assistance (☎ 104). If the car is hired, follow the instructions given in the documentation; most of the international rental firms provide a rescue service.

PERSONAL SAFETY

Greece is one of the safest countries in the world and you are unlikely to experience any problems. Nevertheless, crime has increased in recent years, which the Greeks blame on Albanian immigrants. Mostly this is petty theft, so keep your money and valuables in a money belt or leave them in the hotel safe.

Women travelling alone may be subject to the attentions, wanted or unwanted, of young Greek men known as *kamáki* (harpoonists). Most will stop if you are persistent in your refusals. If attention turns into harrassment, ask the nearest Greek person forhelp. Most Greeks don't like to see this kind of behaviour either.

Tourist Police assistance:
☎ **171**
from any call box

ELECTRICITY

The power supply in Greece is 220 volts AC.
Sockets accept two-pin

round plugs, so an adaptor is needed for most non-Continental appliances and a transformer for appliances operating on other voltages.

TELEPHONES

Most public telephones now accept only phonecards, which are available from kiosks and some shops in units of 100, 500 and 1,000 drachma. An easy option is to use the phone available at most street kiosks, where your call will be metred and you pay in cash. Metred phones are also available

in OTE offices. Some hotels, restaurants, bars and cafés have coin-operated phones, accepting 10-,20-, 50- and 100-drachma coins. To call the operator dial 132.

International Dialling Codes

From Greece to:	
UK:	**00 44**
Germany:	**00 49**
USA:	**00 1**
Netherlands:	**00 31**
Spain	**00 34**

POST

Post Offices
Post Offices (*takhydhromio*) are distinguished by a yellow OTE sign, many cash travellers' cheques and exchange currency: look for the 'EXCHANGE' sign. They are normally open morning shop hours only. Even the smallest Greek island usually has a post office in the main town.

TIPS/GRATUITIES

Yes ✓ No ✗		
Restaurants (service included)	✓	change
Cafés/bars (if service not included)	✓	change
Taxis	✓	change
Tour guides	✓	500dr
Hairdressers	✓	change
Chambermaids	✓	100dr per day
Porters	✓	500dr
Theatre/cinema usherettes	✓	change
Toilet attendants	✓	100dr

PHOTOGRAPHY

What to photograph: The classic sights, markets, Byzantine churches. Look in the harbours for fishermen in their boats or mending their nets. Look for reflections in the water. Deep blue skies and white houses are archetypically Greek.
What not to photograph: Military installations and the police.
When to photograph: Early morning provides the best light. Photograph again when the sun starts to go down.
Where to buy film: Film is readily available from tourist shops but may be of poor quality if it has been stored for some time in the heat

HEALTH

Insurance
Nationals of EU and certain other countries can get medical treatment in Greece with the relevant documentation (Form E111 for Britons), although private medical insurance is still advised and is essential for all other visitors.

Dental Services
Dental treatment is not available free of charge and should be covered by your personal medical insurance. Check with the Tourist Police or with your hotel for the name of the nearest dentist. Dentists are not as widely available in the islands as doctors and pharmacies, so if you are worried you should have a check-up before leaving home.

Sun Advice
The sunniest months are July and August with daytime temperatures well up into the 30s and sometimes over 40°C. Avoid the midday sun and use a strong sunblock. Don't underestimate the dehydrahation effects of walking around sightseeing, and drink lots of water.

Drugs
Prescription and non-prescription drugs and medicines are available from pharmacies (*farmakia*), distinguished by a large green cross.

Safe Water
Tap water is perfectly safe but bottled water is widely available and recommended on islands which suffer water shortages in summer.

CONCESSIONS

Students Holders of an International Student Identity Card (ISIC) are eligible for concessions on travel, museum entrance fees etc.

Senior Citizens The midsummer Greek heat can be insufferable. Consider travelling before July or after mid-September, when the weather will be hot but not deadly. Concessions are available on travel and entrance fees, but you may need to ask and always carry your passport for proof of age.

THE GREEK ALPHABET

The Greek alphabet cannot be transliterated into other languages in a straight-forward way. This can lead to variations in romanised spellings of Greek words and place-names. It also leads inevitably to inconsistencies, especially when comparing different guide books, leaflets and signs. However, the differences rarely make any name unrecognisable. The language looks complex, but it is worth memorising the alphabet to help with signs, destinations etc.

Alpha	Αα	short a, as in hat
Beta	Ββ	v sound
Gamma	Γγ	guttural g sound
Delta	Δδ	hard th, as in father
Epsilon	Εε	short e
Zita	Ζζ	z sound
Eta	Ηη	long e, as in feet
Theta	Θθ	soft th, as in think
Iota	Ιι	short i, as in hit
Kappa	Κκ	k sound
Lambda	Λλ	l sound
Mu	Μμ	m sound
Nu	Νν	n sound
Xi	Ξξ	x or ks sound
Omicron	Οο	short o, as in pot
Pi	Ππ	p sound
Rho	Ρρ	r sound
Sigma	Σσ	s sound
Tau	Ττ	t sound
Upsilon	Υυ	ee, or y as in funny
Phi	Φφ	f sound
Chi	Χχ	guttural ch, as in loch
Psi	Ψψ	ps, as in chops
Omega	Ωω	long o, as in bone

- Remember to confirm your flight details at least three days before departure, and leave a contact number with the airline in case of late changes.
- If travelling on a charter flight, be prepared for delays in the summer months. Have drinks and snacks handy, or enough Greek money left over to buy some.
- If you need to take a ferry to the nearest airport, check weather conditions, likely delays or cancellations

LANGUAGE

The Greek language can look daunting, and certainly sounds it because the Greeks speak with a machine-gun rapidity. It is worth trying to learn a few basic courtesy phrases, though, as the Greeks themselves know how difficult their language is and appreciate the visitor's attempts to learn some. It is also worth trying to memorise the Greek alphabet (► 123) as this can be very useful in reading street signs, bus destinations and so on.

hotel	xenodhohío	chambermaid	kamaryera
bed and	thomatio meh	bath	banyera
breakfast	proino	shower	doos
single room	monoklino	toilet	tooaleta
double room	diklino	balcony	balkoni
one person	ena atomo	sea view	vthea ti
one night	mia nikhta		thalasa
reservation	mia kratisi	key	klidhí
room service	servis thomatiou	lift	asanser

bank	trápeza	exchange rate	sinalagmatiki
exchange office	sarafiko		isotimia
post office	takhithromio	commission	parangelia
coin	kerma	charge	
banknote	khartonomisma	cashier	tamias
cheque	epitayi	change	resta
travellers' cheque	taxithiotiki epitayi	foreign	khartonomismes
credit card	pistotiki karta	currency	xenes

café	café	starter	proto piato
pub/bar	bar	main course	kirio piato
breakfast	proino	dessert	glikisma
lunch	yévma	the bill	logariasmos
dinner	mesimeriano	beer	bira
table	trapezi	wine	krasi
waiter	garsón	water	nero
waitress	garsona	coffee	café

aeroplane	aeropláno	single ticket	apio
airport	aerodhrómio	return ticket	isitirio met
train	treno		epistrofis
bus	leoforio	non-smoking	khoros ya mi
station	stathmós		kapnizondes
boat	plio	car	aftokínito
port	limani	bus stop	stasi leoforiou
ticket	isitirio	where is...?	pou einai...?

yes	neh	excuse me	signomi
no	óchi	you're welcome	parakalo
please	parakalo	how are you?	pos iseh?
thank you	efharisto	do you speak	milate Anglika?
welcome	kalos irthate	English?	
hello	ya sas	I don't understand	dhen katalaveno
goodbye	adio	how much?	poso?
good morning	kalí mera	open/closed	aniktos/klistos
good evening	kalí spera	today	simera
good night	kali nichta	tomorrow	avrio

Acknowledgements

The Automobile Association would like to thank the following photographers and libraries for their assistance in the preparation of this book.

MARY EVANS PICTURE LIBRARY 11, 14b; M GERRARD 76b; INTERNATIONAL PHOTOBANK F/Cover (d) Man in National costume, 5b, 41; JUST GREECE PHOTO LIBRARY/T HARRIS 17b, 79b; MRI BANKER'S GUIDE TO FOREIGN CURRENCY 119; NATURE PHOTOGRAPHERS LTD 12b (J Sutherland), 13a (N A Callow), 13b (R Tidman); PICTURES COLOUR LIBRARY LTD 21b, 39b, 40b; WORLD PICTURES 52b, 63b.

All remaining pictures are held in the Association's own library (AA PHOTO LIBRARY) with contributions from the following photographers: S L DAY F/Cover (a) man painting boat, 1, 2, 5a, 6a, 6b, 7a, 8a, 8b, 8c, 9a, 10a, 12a, 14a, 15b, 16b, 20b, 22b, 23b, 25b, 27a, 28, 29, 72, 75b, 78, 82b, 83b, 84, 85b, 86, 87c, 88, 88/9, 117a, 122c; D HANNIGAN 122b; T HARRIS F/Cover (c) Thira church, (e) mosaic, B/Cover plums, 7b, 9b, 10b, 15a, 16a, 17a, 18a, 19a, 19b, 20a, 21a, 22a, 23a, 24a, 24b, 25a, 26a, 36b, 56, 57, 58, 59a, 60, 61a, 61b, 62a, 62b, 63a, 64, 65a, 65b, 66, 67a, 67b, 68, 69, 70a, 70b, 71a, 71b, 80b; T LARSEN-COLLINGE 27b, 73, 74, 75a, 76a, 77a, 79a, 80a, 82a, 83a, 85a, 87a, 87b, 91a, 92/116, 117b; R MOORE 9c, 42, 54, 81, 90; S OUTRAM 30, 122a; K PATERSON 77b; A SATTIN F/Cover (b) Zakynthos Cave, 18b, 31, 32, 33a, 33b, 35a, 36a, 37b, 38a, 39a, 43, 45a, 45b, 46a, 46b, 47a, 48, 50a, 50b, 51a, 51b, 52a, 53, 55a; J A TIMS 34, 35b, 38b, 47b, 49, 55b; P WILSON 26b, 37a, 44, 91b.

Copy editor: Sarah Boas   Page layout: Jo Tapper